261

HUMAN FUTURE?

HUMAN FUTURE?

Living as Christians in a high-tech world

ALAN JIGGINS

Scripture Union
130 City Road, London EC1V 2NJ

© 1988 Alan Jiggins

First published 1988

ISBN 0 86201 384 4

All rights reserved. No part of this publication may be reproduced, stored in a retrieval system, or transmitted, in any form or by any means, electronic, mechanical, photocopying, recording or otherwise, without the prior permission of Scripture Union.

All Scripture quotations in this publication are from the Holy Bible, New International Version. Copyright © 1973, 1978, International Bible Society.

British Library Cataloguing in Publication Data

Jiggins, Alan
Human Future?: Living as Christians in a high-tech world.
1. Society – christian viewpoints
I. Title
261

ISBN 0–86201–384–4

Phototypeset by Input Typesetting Ltd, London
Printed and bound in Great Britain
by Cox and Wyman Ltd, Reading.

Contents

Preface

It is, I suppose, a common experience among authors to find that the book they have produced has turned out rather differently to the one they had imagined they were going to write. This one is no exception.

As author, I must certainly take responsibility for the main ideas expressed in this book but of course very many people have contributed in one way or another to the final result. I feel the list of credit titles should follow the fashion of today's television and cinema productions and include, for example, all those who have read the manuscript and suggested amendments to it throughout the various editorial stages, and many others who have played an unconscious part in the development of these ideas.

I hope that those who read this through to the end will be provoked to think about the world in a new way. Also, that they will be stimulated to seek answers to questions that do not often seem to be asked.

Alan Jiggins

Foreword

Something has gone drastically wrong with the outlook of our Western culture. Alan Jiggins puts his finger on one of the main problems: 'belief in the power of technology alone to bring us the good life'. For this he uses the term 'technicism' and shows how it is linked with 'the conviction that man is autonomous and at the control of spaceship Earth'.

He argues that we are not always aware of the influence of this pervasive 'faith' in science and technology. Christians, for instance, may be trapped into it when they substitute medical technology for patient care and 'church growth' technology for biblical priorities, or judge success by numbers, efficiency or profitability. If this 'faith' leads the non-Christian into a form of idolatry, it can also lead the Christian to develop a two-compartment mind where his or her religious life is isolated from the secular life in which this outlook is allowed to rule. The questions Alan Jiggins raises are different from those of the secularisation debate and he ends with some positive guidelines for action.

The author is not at all against technology as such, nor its development. He has spent most of his life in technological education (in Applied Nuclear Physics!) and is certainly not apologetic about that. Indeed he is concerned amongst other things for a truly Christian approach to technology. His knowledge of the world of computers and other high-tech developments gives a particularly useful input to the discussion. He can tread with confidence where many others can only speak at second hand.

Some people are now reacting against science and technology, but they usually have little to put in its place and it is still true that from the popular level, in schools and media, upwards this idolatry of technology is still very much alive and influential. If it is not everywhere the most popular alternative to Christian faith, it is still a powerful force which needs to be exposed for what it is and countered in effective ways.

Oliver R Barclay

Introduction

This book is about the society in which we live and the way it is being shaped by technology. Technology is no longer just a matter of 'hardware' like computers or robots; it has revolutionized our way of thinking. A technological attitude is affecting our private ambitions, our social organizations and our relationships with each other. For society as a whole and for most individuals in it the ultimate authority, the ultimate standard and the ultimate solution are now technological in character. We will define this attitude as *technicism*. Just as *humanism* describes faith in man and his self-sufficiency, so technicism describes faith in the ability of technology to solve all our problems. *Technology* simply denotes the 'hardware'. Technicism is the faith which, in most of our public and private life, has replaced faith in God.

In Part One we look at the way this has happened, with examples from very varied aspects of modern life. Think of it rather like a nature trail. Once you have been shown what to look for it is fairly easy to find many other examples for yourself. Taken one at a time each situation may seem harmless and easily justified: it is a more economic way of doing things, it gives higher standards, it saves time, it is a natural development of what has been happening for years. Taken all together, just like the ecology of the nature trail, every small detail is seen to be interdependent and we begin to see the direction in which society is developing.

In Part Two there is some rather more detailed analysis of our technological society. We might describe it as aggressive, machine-minded and double-glazed. It is aggressive because man has assumed the role of master, usurping the authority of God. It is machine-minded because we have redefined truth: we will only admit to something being true if it can be measured and understood by our finite, logical minds. It is double-glazed by our restricted ideas of what can be known, so shutting out the voice of God. The Christian truths on which our society's values have largely been based are being replaced with technological truths and values which are only relative, transient and man-made.

As Christians living in this society we have a mission to fulfil. It is to bring the presence of God into a society which is rapidly losing its sense of need. Part Three examines how we might, as individuals, be rather better at doing this than we are at present. We have to find more direct ways of bringing the sanctifying presence of the Holy Spirit into our technological society. In those small, local areas of life with which we are familiar we can show that the gospel is relevant to today's world.

My intention is not to provide neatly pre-packaged answers. There are many problems which need to be addressed but we will only do so if we ask the right questions. This book, therefore, will provoke you into thinking about modern life in a way you have probably never done before. Most of us have been fed 'answers' for many years, but that does not seem to have got us very far in our job of mission. It is time, therefore, to take a fresh look at the questions and to do some creative thinking about the situation in which we find ourselves.

PART ONE

Overview of a technological society

1

Everything is changing

What's the problem?

Imagine the Good Samaritan travelling down the fast lane of the motorway in the year AD 2000. Just ahead of him three cars smash into each other. The streams of traffic jostle about and slowly converge into one lane as they filter past the tangled chaos. Somebody ought to stop, he thinks, but how – with half a mile tail-back already forming? Better to press on till the road is clear again and then pull over to the hard shoulder.

A quick jog back two hundred yards and our Samaritan arrives to find one driver in a badly wrecked car, nursing a broken arm and a bleeding head. What can he do, his first-aid kit two hundred yards away? Just then, wailing sirens announce the motorway police, alerted by the overhead television monitoring system. One of them applies first aid to the injured driver while the other takes his personal identification card and radios details to the hospital emergency service. Within minutes an ambulance is on its way. A trained casualty nurse has collected a computer printout of the patient's health record, highlighting any special problems such as a history of heart disease or high blood pressure, and any known reactions to drugs. The casualty's blood group is known and transfusion equipment is on board. The computer has already initiated the process of contacting relatives, employer, the DHSS and the tax authorities.

The injured man looks helpless and worried against a background of flashing amber lights and the chatter of non-stop messages on the police radio. Our Samaritan smiles encouragingly at the dazed driver but feels like a useless bystander as he watches the high technology emergency service in action.

'Better get moving again now sir, your car shouldn't be parked on the hard shoulder any longer. Thank you for stopping to help, but everything is taken care of.'

The Samaritan walks back to his car. Well, he did try to help but there was really very little he could do. Thank goodness there is such an efficient system for coping with all the consequences of these accidents! At least, it's good to know that we do help – paying our taxes to make it possible.

Bewildering novelty

All of us have at some time or another experienced that feeling of powerlessness when confronted with a large bureaucratic organization or the latest example of high technology in action. We cannot help but be conscious that we live in a technological world. Our daily papers and the television continually remind us of its effects. We have become blasé about what can be done, and apprehensive or excited, depending on our prognosis, about what *will* be done. Space launches and computer jargon have become part of everyday life. They no longer excite special notice. Embryo manipulation and the totally micro-chip home are almost here. For many of us anticipation is tinged with regret. We mourn the loss of a more predictable world. We are alarmed by the insistent questioning to which our traditional values are subjected.

Has technological man opened up Pandora's Box? If so, what sort of gifts are coming out of it, and what is the nature of their giver? The assertion of this book is that our technological ability is a gift from God, to be used responsibly as part of our stewardship of his creation. To misuse that stewardship is just as much a temptation of the devil as it was in Eden. Giving in to that temptation means that, as a society, we are progressively isolating ourselves from God.

God is replaced

By and large, Western society does not acknowledge that God's truth should be the guiding principle for our lives. People are not aware of God's presence. The predominant attitude is that we are the masters of a closed world. We have finally rejected the possibility that the Lord of the vineyard is going to return for an accounting. There is no Lord; the vineyard is ours to do with as we like. Ethical systems and moral values may provide a useful working hypothesis to help us cope temporarily, and a formal nod to religious ideas is still a valuable focus of unity on formal occasions. But in the final analysis, we believe everything should be subjected to the study and control of science.

We have put all our hopes into the idea of technological progress. We have made it a twentieth-century idol. Many of the leaders in our society today, followed by the great majority of people, accept that this is how things should be. The idea of technological progress motivates all our endeavours; it is the framework within which everything else finds meaning and purpose. In an act of faith we commit everything to it.

The task ahead

Christians who live in a pagan society feel culture shock. It was true in Canaan and in Corinth, and it is true in Britain today. In this book we will look at the fundamental reasons for that culture shock and will attempt to draw up the spiritual battlelines in today's technological world. The task is to convince our society that technical progress is *not* humanity's supreme adventure. We must find practical ways of bearing witness to the truth that our deepest problems cannot be solved by technological methods, because they call for repentance and for reconciliation with an almighty God. We need to make a start on reclaiming for God areas of life where he has been assumed to have little relevance. Today, we must begin to use the whole range of our working experience to speak prophetically. As James Houston expresses it:

> 'A new missionary enterprise is involved: to go virtually into every professional area of life just as in the past we have emphasized the geographical penetration of our world with the gospel.'

Society today

For the great majority of us, our full-time service for God is carried out in the secular world, a world which organizes itself without God. We need to alert each other to the assumptions being made and the values being adopted in this technological society. We need, also, to support each other in the task of sustaining a Christian presence in society, of being ambassadors for Christ.

First of all, we shall take a closer look at what is happening.

The restless society

Most of us who have grown up in or adapted to the industrialized West have learned to live with its inbuilt dynamism: the restless urge to progress and the excitement of living at the frontiers of knowledge. Modern science arose out of a society rooted firmly in a Judaeo-Christian religious tradition. A distinguishing characteristic of this theology is that it is rooted in *time*. It teaches that the world has a specific beginning, a progressive development, a future hope and a culmination in glory. But the sense of time can equally be a threat, a constraint with which we constantly struggle. Andrew Marvell, a seventeenth-century English poet, expressed it like this:

> 'But at my back I always hear
> Time's winged chariot hurrying near.'

And Francis Bacon, an early philosopher of science, like this:

> 'The human understanding is unquiet, it cannot stop or rest and still presses onward but in vain. . . . Our spirits are obsessed by . . . the shortness of life.'

In the West we see the pressure of time as normal. We take it for granted. But it is not the same in all cultures. There are societies which would never have produced writing like that of Marvell or Bacon; time is not a crucial factor in their decision-making or activity. The restlessness of our culture produces extraordinary levels of achievement but it also contains within itself a destructive force. The *status quo* is always under threat, nothing is sacred except the ideology of progress.

The third wave

The present-day situation has been described in a number of books, one of the best-known being *Future Shock* by

Alvin Toffler, an American sociologist. In a subsequent book, *The Third Wave*, he puts forward a model to help us visualize what is happening. Major eras in our civilization are pictured as waves. Initially they move slowly like an ocean swell, but become higher and move faster as they approach the shoreline and finally dissipate themselves on the beach in a thunder of churned-up pebbles and a mist of flying spray. Even as the effect of the breaking wave is being lost in the undertow its replacement is already gathering force for a similar assault. Toffler identifies three successive major waves in our history: the first wave of the agrarian economy, the second wave of the industrial revolution and now, in the process of breaking upon us, the third wave of a post-industrial society.

Most of us will have understood something of the trauma experienced by people who lived through the period of transition between the first and second waves. A society which was structured around farming and rural life was strained almost to breaking point by the industrial revolution. The tensions were economic, social and psychological. In the well-worn phrase, nothing would ever be the same again.

We are now living at a time when the wave model is being re-run. We are living in the last throes of an old civilization and experiencing the birth pangs of the new. We are caught in the backwash and battering pull of the receding second wave at the same time as we are experiencing the thrill and excitement of the approaching third wave. The result is all too obvious to each one of us. In our personal lives we suffer confusion, anguish and disorientation. In wider society we see incoherence in political life, conflict in social relationships and spiritual emptiness. We are the victims of 'future shock'.

Ocean waves begin far beyond our horizons and may take a long time to travel to us, yet once they come within our view their effects are upon us with devastating force. It is a good analogy. The foundations of the third wave revolution which is now upon us were laid many years ago. Some foundational pieces, like Schockley's invention of the transistor, were built upon patiently and unobtrusively for years in laboratories around the world. Another, operational research, began in the 1940s as an attempt to apply scientific method to the process of human decision-making – and the 1950s saw the first commercial use of computers.

Many more key factors have contributed to the present third wave situation, producing an overall picture of extreme diversity and complexity. The complexity and diversity are part and parcel of our present situation. The causes are all interconnected. We cannot (except in the very short term) isolate specific problems in order to solve them with a 'technological fix'.

A new system of values

Toffler believes that people react to this constant change in one of three ways. 'Second wave' people are committed to maintaining a dying order; 'third wave' people to constructing a radically different tomorrow; while the rest are a confused, self-cancelling mixture of the two. Is Toffler correct in identifying a new, third-wave civilization? Will this 'post-industrial' society be radically different from that of the first half of the twentieth century? Or will it evolve by stages in a way we can understand and to which we can adapt? A strong case can be argued from both sides. What is universally agreed, however, is that people, individually and collectively, are under pressure to a degree that has not been experienced before. This is partly due to the *pace* of change to which we are being subjected, and to the *scope* of the changes we are being asked to assimilate. What I believe to be more fundamental to the pressure is the *extreme technological bias* in every aspect of our society. This is subtly changing our value system, infecting personal relationships, and challenging the personhood of men and women.

A watershed of change?

A former Archbishop of York, Stuart Blanch, claims in *The Sound of the Trumpet in the Morning* that many people feel that the late twentieth century is somehow special, that it marks a break with the past. What makes it special is our unique knowledge and our vested interest in change.

But is our situation today so very different from that of the eighteenth-century industrial revolution? Then, within a generation, people were transferred from a restricted, village lifestyle to the open-ended experiences of an urban, industrial economy. A new world of possibilities was opened up. At the same time barriers which were psychologically protective were broken down. Are we today part of a generation living through a cycle of change similar to that described in our history books? Or are we participating in a radically new experience with no precedents and no guidelines, a watershed of change?

A self-destructive society

In his book *Tools for Conviviality*, Ivan Illich, a sociologist and radical critic of modern society, claims that we have reached a watershed because the growth of our organizations has exceeded a natural scale. When that happens, they overwhelm the society that they were designed to serve and become a threat to society itself. He argues that this natural scale is breached when the techniques of mass production become oppressive. We see this in industry when techniques of mass production make skill and craftsmanship redundant; and in schools which are too big for children to have a sense of identity and belonging. The free use of natural ability is extinguished, people are isolated and the texture of community is undermined by social division and extreme specialization. It is in this sense that we can speak of society being self-destructive.

A continual acceleration in the rate of change has

brought us to an acute situation. As a society we can no longer rely on legal, cultural, economic and political precedents to guide us. They are no longer adequate for our situation. Donald Schon, a prominent American technologist, pointed out in the 1970 Reith Lectures that this shortening time scale means that adaptation cannot occur 'naturally' with each generation. Death used to play an essential role in the evolution of societies. The eldest son could introduce new ideas and techniques which his retiring father would have found impossible to implement. Now, change and conflict must be handled within one generation. We are no longer able to afford the relatively leisurely process of adaptation which, until now, has allowed us to keep the illusion of living in a stable society.

A self-reproducing technology

Why, we may ask resentfully, is this happening to us? What have we done to deserve this uncomfortable situation? One answer is that the latter part of the twentieth century has seen the invention of 'meta-technologies' or supervising technologies. These are techniques which enable greater technological innovation, and so increase technological change. For example, information processing has made it possible to collect and manipulate data on a scale unthinkable twenty-five years ago. This means that the pace and scope of invention can now be much better planned and organized. Government and industry have exploited this in order to channel science and technology in specific political and commercial directions. Even in universities, academic freedom to pursue independent research is severely restricted by financial controls. The caricature of a slightly dotty college professor who lives in a dream world, instinctive serendipity his only creed, is long out of date.

Operational research and management science have brought about the ability to manipulate people on a massive scale. Most of us are completely unaware of the extent to which this is possible, and those who exercise the controls do not advertise the fact.

At the core of these meta-technologies are two essential pieces of hardware: the micro-chip and the computer. But they are not to be blamed for the situation in which we find ourselves. Rather, we need to look at the motives and methods of those who use them. Then we will be led to more fundamental answers to the questions of how and why we have got into this situation.

A society centred on organization

So, we are being asked to adjust to an ever-increasing *rate of change* and to a radically different *type of social control*. We shall see that this transition is much more far-reaching than earlier transitions. It does not ask that we simply adapt to different machines or changes in social patterns (eg in employment); but it asks us to change the mental framework that makes our environment coherent. We will have to grasp new ideas of time and space, new systems of organizing knowledge and education. We will have to develop a different relationship to machines. They are no longer simply tools to augment our natural abilities but are becoming more like robots which have different, complementary abilities to our own.

We are suffering from information overload, submerged under a heap of undigested experiences and a flood of half-understood ideas. The boredom and apathy which many of us feel today may be an instinctive defence mechanism, letting us know that we are being asked to carry too much. Perhaps you feel as if you are the wheelbarrow in a wheelbarrow race. You are made to go too fast, you have no choice of direction and it's your hands which get dirty.

The desire to control

Technology today presents us with a challenge to our values, our relationships and our lifestyle. It is no longer just applied science in the form of machines, gadgets and production processes. Today's technology is a way of thinking – about our economics, our social services, our industrial relations, our medical care, our family life. The assumption behind it is that every area of life can be measured, controlled and utilized, including those areas which, until recently, have been considered very individual and personal.

The control of nature

We can trace the origins of this way of thinking to the Renaissance and Leonardo da Vinci's visionary designs of machines for subduing nature. In the following decades the foundations of modern scientific method were laid. Galileo submitted nature to the laws of geometry and brought dogmatic theology before the bar of experimental observation. Descartes put man at the centre of the world, the subject to which all being is related, and he looked out on what he considered to be a purely mechanical world, a vast, intricate clockwork mechanism.

The consequences of this mechanistic view of nature are still with us today. Nature has become an instrument for our use, to be quantified and used objectively. Man started by using scientific methods to observe nature. From there he proceeded to view nature merely as a mechanism, to be manipulated and modified for his convenience. More recently an exciting vision of Utopia has been put before us by such phrases as, 'the white-hot technological revolution' and, 'the great society'. Though these catchphrases are now somewhat tarnished, the underlying assumption remains: man's bias towards goodness will become obvious if only the environment is good, and the environment becomes good if man moulds it to his requirements. It is only too clear that this is proving to be a mirage.

The control of society

So technology colours our view of nature and our relationship to it. But it affects more than that. Descarte's view of nature did not draw a clear line between nature and the person. Experimental science has concluded that human beings are made of precisely the same stuff as everything else and that they too can be be understood as mechanisms. Thus, man is master of society as well. Bertrand Russell, a humanist philosopher, said that society has to be arranged as carefully as a steam engine. With current developments in bio-engineering technology we can look forward to man taking control of his own evolution, perhaps in our lifetime.

Technological thinking is very powerful. We find it attractive because it appeals to our deep materialistic instincts. And it does, after all, deliver some of the goods. However, only a brief look at any major technology will show how much pressure is brought to bear on us to bias our attitudes.

Consider, for example, all the information that comes to us about the car. Is it evenly weighted between benefits and liabilities? Are we given information in a way that will enable us to make an unbiased choice of options? Or are we pressurized into accepting that a continued increase in private transport is inevitable? The associated high accident risk, pollution and extravagance are conveniently overlooked. This example illustrates the power of technology as a driving force in our society. Control over nature, society and man himself has become an idol which we worship.

The faith of technicism

In his book *On Being a Christian* Hans Küng, the contemporary Roman Catholic theologian, argues that we must give up any ideology of technological progress which depends on the notion that human beings can be in total control of the world. Küng is not saying we should give up our concern with human material progress through science and technology. What we must abandon is a belief in science and technology as the only guides to reality and the only criteria for progress. Egbert Schuurman, professor of Philosophy at the Free University of Amsterdam, sees this urge towards technical control as the fundamental motivating power of present-day thinking and action. Technicism is, he claims, the faith of our technological culture.

2

The threats

Invention is the mother of necessity

If we do not abandon our misplaced faith that technology will solve all our problems, our lives will increasingly be ordered on the basis of a value system with which many people would fundamentally disagree. It will become the dominant value system simply because we do nothing to challenge it. Let us consider just a few examples that show how our value judgements have been distorted.

In medicine

Modern medicine is now a technological industry. Progress is measured by standards such as the survival time of organ transplants, the rising capital cost of new therapies and intensive care units, and the cost-effectiveness of particular administrative systems. Meanwhile the waiting lists for hernia and hip replacement operations grow longer and the time that a consultant can give to a patient with an 'ordinary' illness is reduced to a few minutes. We can accept that there is a limit to the resources available, and choosing priorities in a sensitive area will always be like walking in a minefield. But we should ask questions about the criteria on which these priority decisions are made. Is it as easy to obtain funds for work in geriatrics as for heart transplants? If not, why not? What is the value system influencing such decisions? Does the technological glamour of some areas of research give people working in those fields extra clout in the corridors of power?

In education

Education has become a mass industry, organized and guided by technological values. The root meaning of the word 'education' is 'to draw out', but technicism has perverted it to mean 'to pour in'. The technical requirements of industry and commerce are having a heavy influence in the design of courses in higher education, and increasingly in schools. The 1986 Green Paper on Education deals primarily with economic needs and manpower requirements rather than educational opportunities. Its emphasis is on the need to train specialists who will restore our economic fortunes. The cost effectiveness of the people being educated is to be measured by criteria such as success in obtaining jobs and the relative salaries of graduates and non-graduates. The purpose of education now seems to be to turn people into a new type of 'techno-person'.

In industry

I have deliberately chosen non-industrial activities to illustrate the pervasiveness of technicism but, of course, high-tech industry is built solidly upon the faith. The important thing to note is that major industrial development today is led by technology. This is a different situation from that of the industrial revolution, when technology was developed largely in response to an economic need. Then, for example, a growing population at home and colonial development abroad gave rise to an expanding market for cheap cotton and woollen goods. This in turn led to the growth of the industrial mills. In contrast, much of today's new technology comes out of the research programmes of government and industry – research programmes which aim to increase either commercial exploitation or political power. The two are often inextricably mixed. The value system on which decisions are based is either one of economic return or of military security.

The micro-electronics industry with its dazzling display of hardware has become an uncontrollable institution in our society. Ways in which its findings may be applied queue for attention in industrial research laboratories. The gestation time for a new product is many years and the pace of its development is carefully controlled. One of the vital decisions is the date of the market launch. The new product must not be overshadowed by the launch of a competitor's product. On the other hand, it would be economically foolish to bring it out before the market is reaching saturation with an old one. If the product is new, consumer interest must be stimulated first to ensure a good take-off for sales.

The sort of questions that do not get asked are those such as: is the product likely to increase human happiness? Does it meet a human need? What side effects might it have on our social life and individual attitudes? This type of question is ruled 'out of order' by technicism. Instead, previous progress is used as the rationale for further development; nothing less than 'more and more' is considered worthwhile; and the cure for technologically produced problems is more technology. Illich calls this an attempt to solve a crisis by escalation.

When one has become aware of technicism it is easy to see its effects on every area of our life. We look for technical perfection first; other considerations are secondary. So financial speculation changes works of art into objects of art. Compact disc recordings are advertised as giving a quality of reproduction better than the original performance. A large chain of department stores encourages us to buy ourselves a special Christmas present. We are told that one of the most important considerations in planning a major BBC television serial is whether it will sell on the American market. It seems possible to enrol on a course or buy an instruction book for every conceivable activity – bringing up our children, moving into retirement, making love or collecting matchboxes. We are moving into a pre-packaged society where technique delivers the goods to the detriment of involvement, initiative and the unexpected. What effect is this having on relationships in our society?

The worker under threat

Patterns of work have been changing ever since the hunter became the farmer. As society has grown in sophistication, work has become more complex and specialized. E F Schumacher, the economist, originated the concept of 'intermediate technology'. He points out in his book *Good Work* that in spite of the importance of work in our lives, the question of what work does to the worker is frequently overlooked. It is asked by the industrial psychologists and sociologists, but their findings are not always acted upon.

The role of the worker

Schumacher suggests three purposes of work:

1. To provide necessary and useful goods and services.
2. To enable us to use and perfect our talents.
3. To do so in service to and in co-operation with others, so as to liberate ourselves from our inborn egocentricity.

But modern industrial society encourages greed and envy. It depends on incentives which pander to egotism. R H Tawney, the social historian, talks of a system which stunts personality and corrupts human relations. By stunting personality he means that in much modern work there is no worthy challenge, no stimulus to self-perfection, no element of beauty, truth or goodness. Now Tawney and, to a lesser extent, Schumacher were considering work in an industrial society, but their criteria for good work are valid in a third wave, post-industrial society. What is work like in our society, and how does it measure up to the criteria of Tawney and Schumacher?

Sociologists have, for a long time now, been pointing to the emergence of a new society, one characterized by change from an economy which produces goods to one which provides services. There are more professional and technical workers and fewer manual, industrial workers. So-called 'white collar' workers come to dominate the job scene. The trend is clearly reflected in Britain today – in, for instance, changes in trade union membership figures. But has it, in practice, dramatically changed the character of work? David Lyon, a British sociologist and Christian writer on contemporary secular society, doesn't think so. He points out that many 'white collar' workers would be getting those collars dirty if they really wore them! Now that cleaners and car mechanics have had their jobs upgraded by renaming them 'maintenance engineers', they fit better into service industry statistics than into the category of 'manual worker'.

Jobs in a service industry certainly sound as if they ought to be able to fulfil Schumacher's three purposes rather better than manual jobs, for example on a mass production line. One would imagine they would call for skill on the part of the worker, and the exercise of judgement in catering for individual customer's needs. To a certain extent they do but the long shadow of technicism has reached here as well. 'Service' itself is becoming increasingly automated and standardized; it is no longer actually tailored to the individual customer! Rather, the customer is given a standard range of options from which he must choose. For instance, if we take our car into the local dealers it will probably be plugged in to a diagnostic computer to indicate which unit needs replacing – it is unlikely to be given the attention of a skilled craftsman. Once it is going again, if we drive to a roadside café we are quite likely to find that that is run under a franchise system; very clean, efficient and atmospheric. When we stop again one hundred miles further on, the chances are we will walk into an almost identical establishment, the same menu, the same decor, the same smiles on the faces and the same soap in the wash rooms.

Not only is service becoming more standardized, it shifts more of the responsibility for the work onto those it claims to be serving. The 'service' sector has become the 'self-service' sector. When we fill our car with petrol, take groceries from the supermarket shelves or ferry rubbish to the local tip we are co-operating in a process in which jobs requiring little skill are taken from a paid worker and given to an unpaid one. A technological industry is cutting its costs by reducing its work-force. The advertisements tell us it is in the interests of wider consumer choice and lower prices. How do these developments meet the challenge of Schumacher and Tawney? Who is benefitting from these changes in work patterns?

The dispensable worker

The industrial society is being replaced by the information society. Political and economic power will, in future, rest not primarily with those who produce *things* but with those who are able to process and use *information*. Word processing and data storage are available over the counter of high street shops and we are familiar with computerized invoicing, bank statements, and bar-coding on everything from library tickets to orange squash. Information technology is revolutionizing the commercial office, the management of industry and all aspects of retailing. These are areas where, traditionally, employees were required to exercise some initiative and responsibility. But even here, office automation is at last providing an opportunity to reduce costs and increase control on a scale comparable with that already taking place in manufacturing.

The most painfully obvious symptoms of the changes taking place today are the unemployment figures. Mostly, they reflect the massive decrease in the numbers of people employed in manufacturing industry. In a decade of high inflation and market saturation, industry is again cutting its costs. The first time round it did so by doing away with the time-consuming and unpredictable element of human craftsmanship, and put people on production lines instead. Now it is doing away with the human element altogether: robots, in any shape or form, are much more capital intensive than people but they do what they are told without question, they don't have days off and they don't ask for more pay each year. The move to automation is principally a move towards more control, to a more calculable, predictable world without the uncertainties of human interactions. It is of course true that people who are replaced by robots are being spared the repetitive jobs which leave no room for creativity or initiative. But we must ask whether this is really the result of concern for the worker. If it is, we should be able to see satisfying work being provided in exchange. We rarely do.

People who express alarm at the disastrous psychological and social effects of massive unemployment are assured that the problem is only temporary. We are told that there will be a growth of jobs in the service sector to compensate for those lost in manufacturing, while the new technology of information processing will create more jobs than it destroys, just as other technologies have done in the past. Well, the shift from manufacturing to service is happening, as the weekly television review of job losses and gains shows; but so far it has only had a slight effect on total unemployment. Even the most optimistic can only say that the steady fall in total jobs available has bottomed out.

Will the service industry really be able to provide jobs for all those who need them? Surely there must be a limit to the number of new hypermarkets and building society offices that are needed? And even these as we have noted, are themselves being semi-automated by the new technology.

Is there a real prospect that the field of information technology will provide the jobs? Nobody really knows but some clues may be found in an anlaysis of recent employment figures from the United States. They show that genuine growth in the information sector provided only a small fraction of the growth required to make a significant impact on structural unemployment. In fact, the majority of new jobs in information technology seem to be located in the Third World, where willing and low-paid workers seem ready to accept the repetitive work involved in the assembly of component parts.

I think it would be fair to conclude that micro-electronic automation is developed primarily for the economic benefits of big industry. It is not designed for the benefit of workers or consumers anywhere in the world in spite of the glossy brochures promising us more leisure, more creative work and wider horizons of communication.

The cult of the specialist

The basic trend common to all industrial and commercial activity is the trend to expand. Progress is measured in terms of increasing sales, bigger profits and more power, leading to a drive to develop more complex machines for faster continuous production. The growing cost of automation has to be paid for and one of the most effective ways is to reduce the number of people employed. Those people who will keep their jobs are either those whose jobs are too low paid to make investment in automation worthwhile, or they are among the small number of specialists who design and implement the new systems. The religion of technicism has a priesthood of specialists. The collective knowledge and traditions of a skilled workforce have been transformed into the property of a technological élite. 'Job enrichment' is only for the few.

This is very obviously the case in high technology factories where a small, highly specialized management continually monitors and controls every aspect of the working day. But it is equally there in other less likely areas. More packaged learning schemes are being produced for schools and higher education; hard-pressed teachers with too little time for preparation gratefully accept this gift from the experts. In retail stores it is becoming increasingly difficult to find staff who know anything about the goods they are selling. They don't need to: stocking is computer controlled and buying is done on a multinational basis by marketing experts. In our National Health Service, confrontation over nursing management continues. In 1987 the Royal College of Nursing mounted a national advertising campaign to protest against the implementation of the Griffiths Report. This report advocated the appointment of general managers to run health service units (hospitals?) more efficiently, with the result that nurses would be excluded from vital management decisions. The Royal College argued that nursing expertise is necessary in many important administrative decisions. The needs of patients are not usually obvious to administrators primarily interested in cost-effectiveness.

The downgrading of skills

Many people regard science and technology with a sort of awe, and many others have an underlying fear of them. Are these sensible attitudes? Are they justifiable? While modern technology is mediated by an élite priesthood and protected by specialist jargon, the average person is less and less able to understand its principles and practices. We are afraid of becoming a machine-dominated society and of losing personal control over our lives. Yet at the same time we seem to have great faith in the power, reliability and desirability of machines. The explosion of the twenty-fifth space shuttle just after launch in 1987, was described on TV news as, 'the accident *that we never thought could happen*'. The assumption behind that statement could not be justified in any rational way. It was, rather, an example of the soothing and reassuring language that is put out to condition the population at large and to suppress our inward doubts at some of the developments being thrust upon us.

Because of our faith in the reliability and desirability of machines, the craftsman is being replaced by the technician. Instead of building up years of experience which allow their talent to develop, people are sent on short courses to learn semi-automatic routines. Work which was formerly highly skilled is being reduced to the correct sequence of button pushing. The reason for this is that the nature of tools is changing.

Ivan Illich points out the dangers in this trend. The craftsman uses tools to enhance his own energy and imagination in a way which meets Schumacher's criteria of good work. But the trend during the last fifty years has been to make machines do the work *instead* of the craftsman. These complex machines are so beyond our individual understanding that we are in danger of becoming enslaved to the systems we have created. And we seem happy to co-operate in the process, though it may substantially reduce our quality of life, because of the dazzling selection of consumer goods offered to us in return.

What is not so readily recognized is that the way we use our tools and machines influences our own self-image. People used to be valued in their local society for their *skills* and their contribution to the community. Modern industrial practice degrades people into users and consumers. In this context we can widen the concept of 'tool' to include institutional tools – the management and organizational structures with which we direct most aspects of our lives. This gives another pointer to technicism being the main driving force of our society.

Consider just two examples of the way in which the type of tool determines the self-image of the person who uses it. Biscuit making used to be a highly skilled and individualistic craft, involving the master baker, the decorators and cutters, the finishers and packers. To reach for bigger markets, production has now been standardized and detailed cost control established. Almost every stage of the process is now fully automated and biscuits are made by the multimillion without any exercise of skill or judgment on the part of the machine operators. The only part of the process still too expensive to automate is the final packing, so this is still done by hand using the cheapest labour available (100 per cent women, mostly part-time). Now the decisions on the best way to make biscuits are logically unchallengable within the terms of reference of the present economic system. But the social cost is very high.

Some people have had almost all opportunities for judgment and responsibility removed from their work. Many others have been made redundant, with the message that society has no further need for their contribution. There are also those who have to learn to live with the insecurity of part-time and casual employment. They know that they are thought of in similar terms to a production machine that can be switched on or off as required.

We do not have to go to a traditional craft industry to find other instances of the degrading of people's skills. Take computer programming as our second example. This was initially thought to be unskilled and routine work and programmers were predominantly female. With the development of large-scale systems and the increasing capacity of dedicated micros programming became highly skilled and therefore male dominated and highly paid. However we are now seeing the concept of 'structured programming' being developed: packages are picked from a library shelf and linked together. Programme-writing programmes are also being produced: the computer itself is instructed to do most of the work. The status of the average computer programmer is, consequently, being reduced again and the expected economic signs are there: lower pay and a female workforce.

So we see that status in society can change because of the tools we design and use. Trades unions usually argue for a higher value to be placed on workers who use advanced technology because they are involved in higher productivity. Management often appears to give them a lower value. It treats workers as just part and parcel of the production process; they seem to be equated with the machinery, to be used and discarded as techniques change. The individuals themselves are often confused and discouraged by changes totally outside their control. Retraining can bring hope and respect; redundancy can result in a deep sense of worthlessness.

Technicism is a force for change in very many areas of our working lives, either as employees or as customers. The concept is based on a philosophical idea known as reductionism: the breaking down of a complex problem into the smallest possible parts, so that it can be analysed and controlled. It is the traditional method by which Western science operates and, as we all know, it has produced astonishing results. As a scientific method with clearly defined limits it has tremendous power. But if adopted as a philosophy, in the belief that it can give complete answers to human problems, it will lead us to form an environment which is not responsive to basic human needs.

Leisure under threat

According to the optimists we are about to enter the age of leisure. If it is true it will be one of the most dramatic social changes ever experienced by the human race. Will a new generation of machine slaves really relieve us of the need to spend most of our time earning a living? Will we welcome it when it happens or will we then need to learn how to kill time when we have nothing useful to do? The attitudes of trades unions and employers to the prospect do not seem very positive. There seems to be very little serious discussion about job sharing or the creation of a shorter working week, let alone more radical restructuring of our concept of work. Individually, many welcome the chance to work overtime. The black economy is thriving with people doing a second job and the DIY boom shows no sign of running out of steam. Schumacher has commented that, paradoxically, the amount of genuine leisure available in society is generally in *inverse* proportion to the amount of labour-saving machinery it employs. Owning a car does not seem to make more time available at the end of the day. We just pack more activity into the same few hours. Quite apart from the amount of leisure we enjoy, the way in which we spend it is being transformed.

> 'He had just come to the bridge and not looking where he was going he tripped over something and the fir-cone jerked out of his paw into the river. 'Bother' said Pooh as it floated slowly under the bridge and he went back to get another fir-cone which had a rhyme to it. But then he thought that he would just look at the river instead, because it was a peaceful sort of day, so he lay down and looked at it, and it slipped slowly away beneath him and suddenly, there was his fir-cone slipping away too. And that was the beginning of the game called Poohsticks which Pooh invented and which he

and his friends used to play on the edge of the Forest.'
(*The House at Pooh Corner*, AA Milne, Methuen.)

Whatever our personal views on the age of leisure, big business is certainly in no doubt that it should have very little to do with floating twigs down a river. It would much rather that young children were taken to the local leisure centre to play in an architect-designed swimming pool complete with wave-making machine and artificial palm beach. Technicism has invaded our leisure and we can see the effects in our sport, hobbies and entertainment.

Sport

As an industry, sport has become its own victim. As with other industries, it requires growth and profits. Sponsorship, investment and calculated business risk have effectively squeezed out the amateur from any sport at national level. Highly professional training and management leads to converging standards of performance and an artificially created competitive tension. Moreover technology has the answer to a technologically induced problem: electronic timing now makes split-second decisions for us that no one simply watching the event can possibly appreciate.

The extent to which individual competition and appreciation of a performance have been downgraded can be seen by what is emphasized in sports reporting: disputes over decisions, drug disqualifications, political exclusions and technical objections. In his book, *Made in America*, Peter Ueberroth describes how the 1984 Olympic games were organized. It is crystal clear that the major problems were those of commercial sponsorship and political persuasion. In the end, the games were reported to have been the most spectacular and successful ever staged – they 'must have been' because they made a profit of 225 million dollars.

Television has completely altered spectator involvement in sport. The zoom lens, action replay and multiple viewing from several cameras have given TV watchers a more precise and reliable view of the action than any referee or umpire can possibly have! This technical advance leads inevitably to dissatisfaction with human decisions. Violence is often the result, as the humans involved in the game still make mistakes. Perhaps we should move to the extreme limit of sporting technology: computer-simulated football and athletics. It would be, after all, only a more sophisticated version of the pools panel that sits in closed session on wet Saturday afternoons!

Hobbies

Hobbies of infinite variety have been our traditional leisure activities. They adapt to all levels of taste, ability and resources, and have given challenge and delight to many people. It was hardly likely that an area of social life so wide open to business opportunity would escape the grip of technicism. Stamp collecting used to be a matter of chatting up local businesses with foreign mail, or advertizing for pen friends abroad. Now it is big business. First-day covers can be sent to you automatically and philatelic sales are a significant part of the budget for some postal services.

Entirely new markets can be created out of the collecting instinct. You may already, in unsolicited mail, have been invited to join the Thimble Collectors Club with an exclusive free gift introductory offer. I am told that through membership of the club I can build an unrivalled collection, month by month, which would be practically impossible to assemble on my own. That's true; many of those thimbles are specially made just for monthly distribution to keep the club members happy. What a perversion of a hobby! There is no thrill of discovery, no memories of the places where items were found, no personal link with those people from whom they were obtained, no challenge to build a collection unique to oneself. Just the routine monthly package and payment by credit card transfer.

Entertainment

Home entertainment has taken off. In the Financial Times in 1978 we were told that the technological invasion of our living rooms had only just begun. As the conventional markets become saturated the electronic industries reach out to our leisure time to find new areas of sale.

The traditional view of leisure as sitting on a river bank quietly fishing, or as having more time talking to our friends, is not the vision of leisure which the micro-electronics industries share. For them leisure provides more time to consume more goods. So information systems originally designed for business use are being pressed onto a gullible public, even though they have no use for most of the information that then becomes available to them. Some computers will process our household accounts and do our tax returns even if most people do not need this level of sophistication or understand the mechanics of it. More intriguingly they offer the prospect of playing computer games. It is not by chance that most of these games involve violent destruction of enemies in some shape or form: research leading to this type of equipment was originally done for military purposes. Computer games were a natural spin-off, and have become a profitable sideline. At least they transfer our aggression from people to impersonal machines; whether that is good for us I would not know.

There may be a more sinister reason for reconstructing our leisure around technology. Playing with computers may be psychologically less disturbing than working with computers. An executive from a major corporation said that resistance to office computers would diminish with the increase of computer games in the home. '. . . We shall be forced to have these games because of our children. The reluctance to use systems in the office will disappear.'

Two American writers, Albury and Schwartz, comment in *Partial Progress* that the makers of home computers have become the new Jesuits. 'Give us a child till the age of seven and he is ours for life.'

3

A God's-eye view

It is time to stand back and make a preliminary Christian assessment of the criticisms being made about our society today. The Bible gives no simple answers but in it there are examples of people who come under pressures similar to those which we face. The temptations raised by materialism, the pride in human achievement, and the desire to be independent are not special to the twentieth century. They are attitudes deeply ingrained in human nature.

The purpose of material goods

Our technological culture is built upon materialism, the desire to possess. It deliberately encourages us to acquire more and more. Jesus told a parable, recorded in Luke 12:16–21, about a man who had a lot of possessions and whose main aim was to increase his wealth even more.

God condemned the man for his greed and foolishness. Many centuries earlier Joseph in Egypt faced a situation not so very different (see Genesis 41:47) and the action he took was apparently rather similar to that of the man in the parable. Joseph, however, was acting with God's approval. What then can we learn from those two examples of coping with a glut of material possessions?

In Luke 12:16–21 we see that this very rich man was entirely self-centred; no other parable of Jesus is so full of the words *I, my, myself*. This man lived in a closed world surrounded by the security fence of his material possessions. They were his source of happiness and the guarantee of his future. But his priorities were wrong. God broke through his security fence and exposed the errors of his thinking. Firstly, he had given priority to the material life in this world and totally ignored the fact that it was on lease from God (v 19). Secondly, he had assumed that time was at his disposal rather than under God's control (v 20). Thirdly, and most crucial of all, *he*, not God, came first in his thinking (v 21). 'Fool' is the word Jesus used to describe him.

Back in Egypt Joseph also stored up his harvests, huge quantities, too much to keep records of (Genesis 41:47–49). How does his action differ from that of the rich man in the parable? Firstly, Joseph was very conscious that God was ordering these events (v 25) and that the ability to cope with such practical situations came ultimately from God. Secondly, Joseph's priorities were such that he listened to God, accepted his guidance and interpreted it with a divinely informed common sense (vs 33–38). Thirdly, his motive for storing up this wealth was to bring economic stability to the country (vs 35–36). This future planning was based not on personal greed but on providing for the community. Incidentally Joseph did very well out of it, but that was not his prime motive in acting as he did. The underlying thought is that God is the prime provider and we are the responsible users. There is no assumption by Joseph of an automatic prosperity, no suggestion of finding ultimate security in material wealth, only a reasonable judgement about how to deal with a few years of famine.

This story also gives us a very striking example of what is involved in working under the guidance of God. Joseph didn't get a set of detailed instructions. He expected to rely on experience, judgment, calculation, conservation of resources, administrative skills and government authority. All of those things were, however, subject to the overall sovereignty of God.

The use of technology

If we look earlier in biblical history we find further examples of the right and wrong use of technology. The people who built the tower of Babel, as told in Genesis 11 seem to have been technologically advanced (v 3). They used their skills for self-aggrandisement, seeking security behind man-made walls and looking for an identity based on their own spectacular achievements (v 4). There is no suggestion that they acknowledged responsibility for, or accountability to, anyone outside their society. They lived in a world with limited horizons. In these circumstances God intervened very directly to prevent an even more critical situation developing, and the whole technological society they had constructed was destroyed.

In contrast to this we see God himself, in Genesis 6, using man's technological skills to retrieve another disastrous situation. God used the technological skills of a man who was righteous and who walked with God to continue the divine plan for creation. Noah built the ark under the guidance and within the will of God. It was not built for the personal status of Noah, nor to satisfy a greedy ambition, but was an integral part of the establishment of God's covenant with man. It was technological skill sanctified for holy use.

The temptations of technicism

Faith in our own, increasing power to control is distorting our value system and fundamentally changing the way we think in every area of our lives. We are being tempted in very subtle ways just as Jesus was in the wilderness. If we read that account in Matthew 4 we will see that, although the techniques of the temptations have changed, the goods on offer are very similar. We are offered a way to meet our genuine needs, to fulfil our desire for power, and to satisfy our greed.

Of course the temptations of Jesus were unique. He had unique powers, and he knew it. And yet there was something in his temptations relevant to all temptation. The writer to the Hebrews, emphasizing the humanity of Jesus, says that he was tempted in every way, just as we are, and yet was without sin. So, the writer continues, he is able to help others who are being tempted.

To meet all needs

In Matthew 4:2–3 we see that the appeal of the devil is to a real, basic need: hunger:

> 'After fasting forty days and forty nights, he was hungry. The temper came to him and said, "If you are the Son of God, tell these stones to become bread." '

The implication was that Jesus had no need to be hungry. He only had to say the word and he could provide a feast for himself, so why not? Many people in the world today have this desperate need and would dearly like to possess that power. In the wisdom of God the power has been given to those who have no need and in our self-centredness we fail to use it. But for us in the West today the temptation has a wider context. Our 'basic needs' seem to increase each year and we assume we have a right to have them fulfilled. We go to our god, technology, and ask him to meet our needs. All we have to do is to set up the research, make the right plans, and form suitable organizations. Jesus' reply to the devil is still relevant. Man does not live by bread alone; his basic needs are important, but they are not the most important things. James Barrie imagined a Peter-Pan world in which the laws of nature could be suspended if one only wished hard enough. Today we are living in a similar situation. Our technological wishing is assumed to dispense with the eternal laws of God.

To pride

Jesus second temptation was to pride:

> 'Then the devil took him to the holy city and made him stand on the highest point of the temple. "If you are the son of God," he said, 'throw yourself down. For it is written:
> 'He will command his angels concerning you,
> and they will lift you up in their hands,
> so that you will not strike your foot against a stone." '
> (Matthew 4:5–6)

A great deal of our society today is maintained by an appeal to our pride. We almost dare ourselves to take another scientific or technological leap forward just for the excitement of it. This is not to say that all ambition and adventure is wrong; we are given a mandate to subdue and enjoy the world. But if this process involves an arrogant pride in our own achievements and an unjustified confidence that we can always find a solution whatever problems we create, then we come under God's condemnation.

To worship our skill

> 'Again, the devil took him to a very high mountain and showed him all the kingdoms of the world and their splendour. "All this I will give you," he said, "if you will bow down and worship me." ' (Matthew 5:8–9.)

Isn't it interesting that this is a gift of the devil not of God? The gift that was offered was magnificent and over-abundant but, like the rather more modest free offers that drop through our letterboxes, there is a hidden price to pay. Bowing down and worshipping means giving one's allegiance; putting someone or something first. This is precisely what technicism encourages us to do. We are encouraged to make an idol of our technical skill and the system we have created, so that it will give us in exchange the benefits of our high standard of living and a promise of unlimited progress. There is the hidden assumption that even our wildest desires will be obtained if we only sacrifice on the altar of more research, more organization, more power, more control.

Although the particular temptations we face today are part of a mass movement that is unique in history, the same basic temptations have been faced by mankind since the dawn of time. Adam and Eve were encouraged to satisfy what seemed to be a legitimate need: the fruit was good for food. The serpent suggested that they could dispense with God's laws, and progress by means of their own strength. He appealed to their pride and ambition. 'You will not surely die', he said. 'For God knows that when you eat it your eyes will be opened and you will be like God.' Again, as with all free offers, this one had a price, that of knowing good and evil. We have been trying to pay off the mortgage ever since. The parallels with modern advertising are quite startling. It has all the same elements: the creation of desire, the suggestion of marvellous new opportunities, the suppression of doubts, the stimulation of appetite through eye appeal, emotional attraction and the promise of power. Finally the whole process is validated with a shared experience.

So we can begin to see that the Bible contains some very relevant comment for our society today. It reveals a fundamental difference between the priorities which emerge as a result of technicism, and those set out for us by God.

We will now try to draw together a picture of the main characteristics of our society today, and contrast that with what we know of God's plan for his creation.

PART TWO

Analysis of a technological society

How have we got to where we are?

How will future historians see the decades in which we are living? What labels will they stick on us in an attempt to give an impression of our society? Without the detachment and broad perspective which they will have, but with the heightened awareness that comes from being in the front line, we will consider three ways of characterizing our society.

Firstly, it is an *aggressive* society. The new technology of today is concerned with knowledge; knowledge confers power, and power gives control. Increasingly we see ourselves as masters rather than stewards, of ourselves and our environment.

Secondly, it is a *machine-minded* society. Our technological mindset makes us look only for technological solutions. We are suffering from tunnel vision.

Thirdly, we live in a man-made world, where what happens is determined by technology. Because we adopt the aggressive attitude of masters and because we have limited our choice of options, we are progressively cutting ourselves off from any experience of the transcendent. Our society is becoming a *double-glazed* society.

4

An aggressive society

Knowledge is power

In society today knowledge is all-important. The key technology in this quest for power via knowledge is information processing. It is a 'supra-technology', one which transforms all other technologies. Information processing is the practical means of centralizing and analysing data. At a humble level we see it available in our new kitchen gadgets and electricity meters. At the level of super-power confrontation Frederick Forsyth in his novel, *The Devil's Alternative*, shows us its frightening scope and power. The president of the United States is looking at a television picture beamed across the world by satellite:

> 'The picture came closer, slower. Against the bole of a lone tree a Russian peasant slowly unbuttoned his fly. President Matthews was not a technical man and never

ceased to be amazed. He was, he reminded himself, sitting in a warm office on an early summer morning in Washington, watching a man urinate somewhere in the shadow of the Urals mountain range.'

Such access to and control of knowledge is, I believe, turning us into an arrogant and exploitative society. Aggressive and invasive power is corrupting our value system. It is subtly changing our relationships. We have been given a Midas touch but, as in the legend, its results can be devastating and unpredictable.

What is man?

The way we think of ourselves and of human society reveals both our value system and the philosophical basis of our thinking. The model is the message. For many centuries in the western world the Judaeo-Christian model of mankind has been dominant. This model describes man as being 'in the image of God' but as fallen from that created perfection. We are created with free will but only in the context of the overriding authority of God.

With the Renaissance this view began to be challenged; man was seen as rational, responsible and autonomous. In the context of industrialization man was often thought of as a producer. Post-industrial prosperity has been built on the idea of man as consumer. Democratic societies give token recognition in varying degrees to man as a free individual; totalitarian societies emphasize man as servant of the state.

What are the modern technological models of man and how do we use them? Psychologists following the lead of Freud often assume that man is basically aggressive and shaped by instinct and childhood experiences. Biological determinists show that genes control behaviour: we are the victims of physiological predestination. Behavioural psychologists believe that we merely react to prods from our enivronment and that self-realization depends on freeing ourselves from ingrained and conditioned responses.

All these models reveal our fascination with the techniques of control and the possible results of using this power. Man is considered to be an adjustable, chemically controlled machine whose psyche can be programmed for specific purposes. Accepting these models of man leads to the concept that human beings are available for manipulation. If we do not function 'normally' then either the hardware (the biological system) or the software (social programming) can be changed and appropriate corrections made. Human beings are assumed to be creatures of almost unlimited plasticity who can be moulded for their own good and for the good of society.

We shall look briefly at three manipulative techniques now in use or being developed, in order to grasp the range of possibilities being opened up by new technology. Then we shall consider the motivation behind this drive to control and, later on, the effect this is having on our view of the status of the human person.

Techniques for manipulating man

Bio-engineering: new genes for old

Molecular biology has taken over from high energy physics as the most newsworthy of the sciences. One reason is that fundamental particle physics has become so mysterious that its practitioners have difficulty in talking to other physicists, let alone to the general public! A more basic reason is that the relevance of the work of such physicists is not immediately obvious to the majority of us. In contrast, the uncovering of some of the mechanisms of human heredity and reproduction have touched a primitive chord in most of us; there is no doubt about their relevance. It has become possible to manipulate the genetic code, control fertilization, screen embryos, and clone cells.

A report published in 1944 recorded the first planned genetic alteration of bacteria, and identified the type of molecule involved. Only nine years later James Watson and Francis Crick put their names on the front pages of our newspapers by throwing light on the detailed structure of DNA. This is the molecule which forms the genetic code for a cell. Since then molecular biologists have developed the capacity not only to observe but also to produce types of DNA not occurring in nature. Man has acquired a power which would previously have been considered either a divine prerogative or the result of chance: the power to design and alter human genetic make-up. On the one hand this gives us grounds to hope for a cure for cancer and genetically inherited illness. On the other hand, it reinforces a mechanistic view of human beings, so strengthening the hold of technicism.

Most of us are aware of the medical technologies based on this fundamental research. They may even be part of our personal experience. They include organ transplants, drugs to modify interactions between cells, and pre-natal diagnosis and treatment. Diagnosis and treatment is the function of medicine and is assumed to be a good thing. But modern techniques are raising moral issues on a scale not previously experienced because our scientific knowledge has given us unprecedented power. But use of this power requires exceptional levels of responsibility. This is perhaps most easily recognized in the area of amniocentesis, the analysis of a sample of the fluid surrounding the embryo. It is now possible to identify chromosome anomalies, enzyme and neural tube defects.

At present this technology is used mainly to help parents decide whether to have an abnormal foetus aborted, but already there are serious suggestions that it should be used for general social control. Do individuals have a right to decide whether to produce children or not, irrespective of the medical problems? Does society and its agent, the government, have a right to interfere with our free choice? In *The People Shapers* Vance Packard gives a wide ranging survey of the techniques of control now being developed. He quotes Bentley Glass, a geneticist, as saying,

> 'Leaders of the future will decree that parents have no right to burden society with a malformed or mentally incompetent child. Future societies will regulate who gets born and who does not. If nothing else, population pressures will make regulation inevitable. The once sacred rights of man must change in many ways.'

This is not a lone, idiosyncratic scientist speaking; control on a mass scale is already being exercised in the birth control programmes of, for example, India. In the case of the implantable chemical contraceptive, Depro Provera, the principle of *informed* consent seems very unlikely to be upheld in the Third World. Long-term consequences and possible side effects are simply not disclosed.

The presence of the XYY chromosome in some males has been thought to correlate with mental retardation and physical violence, that is, to predispose the individual to possible criminal tendencies. It is an example of the biological view of man reinforcing mechanistic thinking: it challenges the environmental explanation for criminal behaviour and also tends to suppress all questions of individual accountability. Whether the correlation is significant or not, and serious doubts have been expressed, the issue has been raised and moral questions follow. Must the parents, and later the individual, be told, or do doctors have a right to withhold the information? The power of such knowledge is incalculable. To what extent does it affect our relationship with that person? To what extent are those with access to this information to control his future? To what extent will that individual be credited with accountability for his own actions?

Some couples run the risk of producing genetically abnormal children. Now that these risks can be identified, should there be a legal restriction on such couples marrying or conceiving children? At least this would avoid the controversial solution of abortion. There are, after all, long-established precedents for such restrictions; putting them on a scientific basis does not change the principle involved. Technology, as so often, suggests an answer: artifical insemination from a donor, with selected sperm, will remove the genetic incompatibilities. The business entrepeneur has already seen a lucrative slot in the market. Sperm from Nobel prizewinners is for sale in the USA.

Our knowledge is giving us increasing power and control over our lives but it is also raising more complex problems. Genetic diagnosis identifies very specifically the variability of human beings and also gives us criteria for establishing the normal. This holds the danger that the unusual is then stigmatized. For example, prospective parents can very easily move from an attitude of using pre-natal diagnosis for specific rare conditions to one of assuming they have a right to a 'normal' child. As in all other fields of research, a rapidly advancing technology raises the level of expectation of what is possible. In research on animals biological engineering has moved from the search for cures to the attempt permanently to modify characteristics thought to be undesirable. Will we be tempted to use our knowledge for the 'improvement' of the human species as well? Eugenics is not a new concept and specific programmes have been attempted in the past for political reasons. More recently it has been suggested that new genes could be introduced into the human stock to enable us to synthesize vitamin C. Decompression before childbirth is claimed to produce more intelligent children, and growth hormones have been used to stimulate brain development before birth.

Technology is certainly not making life any simpler. Our choices are becoming more complex and are revealing tensions between values that we hold very deeply. It would, however, be impractical to try to put a stop to certain types of experimental work. It would also be impossible to renounce the knowledge we have acquired, and unreasonable to reject the many real benefits brought to us by these advanced techniques. But we can and should repudiate technicism, the assumption that the technological answer is the only answer and that the only criteria for progress are those that can be quantitatively measured. Victor Weisskopf, one of the pioneers of nuclear physics, has pleaded for a more balanced philosophy in our scientific age, commenting that, 'Curiosity without compassion is inhuman; compassion without curiosity is ineffective.'

Behaviourism: anyone can be manipulated

Behaviourists, too, look for change and improvement in the human being but approach the problem from a very different perspective. They see the human person as a 'black box', a complex mechanism whose inner workings can be largely ignored but whose behaviour can be influenced by external stimuli. Their model of a person does not include any conscious decision-making capacity, any exercise of free will. The model only *reacts*, in ways that are in principle predictable, to the external environment. It also forms habits of typical reactions to similar stimuli, a process called conditioning. Pavlov, the Russian physiologist, pioneered the investigation of conditioned reflexes in animals and came to attribute all actions to them, including deep personal emotions. B F Skinner is one of the leading modern advocates of conditioning who considers widespread control and programming of people as the best hope for saving the society of the western world. In his book *Beyond Freedom and Dignity* he says that human survival depends upon deciding how people must behave and then using behavioural engineering techniques to see that they do. Man's continuing struggle for freedom does not arise from an inner will but is simply a reaction to unfavourable stimuli. So the treatment is to analyse and change the kind of control or stimuli to which people are exposed.

Skinner's work and ideas have been taken up very widely and the results pervade our society, sometimes in unsuspected ways. Behaviour control techniques are in active use in schools, factories and hospitals. They guide the planning of our social environment, our entertainment, our leisure activities and the production and marketing of most of the goods we purchase. The actual techniques may be as basic and familiar to us as a simple reward system for acceptable behaviour. Are there any parents who have not resorted thankfully to this well-tried approach? But when the method is extended to medical and psychological problems of a serious nature, such as bed-wetting or extreme rebellious behaviour in children, and to social situations such as marriage guidance, the alarm bells begin to ring. Educational techniques use peer pressure and collective reward systems, and many teaching machines are built around the same ideas.

The problem is that while the aims are often good, the technique does work, the approach seems gentle, it must be asked to what extent the end justifies the means. How far should we go in basing our interaction with other people on a philosophy which assumes they are 'black boxes' capable only of reflex reactions? At a practical level there are often serious problems with the temporary nature of the results. Human nature seems to involve increasing expectations and so a reward system must be graded to maintain results. Certainly the retail marketing research people recognize the short term effect of reward systems in their endless round of special offers, designed to maintain brand loyalty. In a much more subtle way the design and furnishing of the stores, the display of merchandise and even the clothes of the sales assistants are all geared to produce a feeling of confidence in the prospective customer. Walk down your local high street and critically examine the total presentation of the health food shop, boutique, supermarket and building society. How are they using behaviour control techniques in their marketing strategies? The variety offered is, of course, genuinely pleasing: we may really enjoy the background music or the modern art on the walls. The danger is that we probably believe it has no influence on our behaviour; a multimillion pound industry disagrees.

Invasive conditioning

Skinner and his followers choose to influence our minds by external stimuli, others have been using more invasive techniques such as drug treatment or electrical stimulation. Alcohol and nicotine have been used socially for so long that most people accept them and their effects without question, as part of normal life. Perhaps for this very reason they form a special case. Certainly the wide range of mood-influencing drugs currently available are much more specific and potent. They also make possible the mass treatment of whole populations, with or without consent. Tranquillizers available for personal use under medical supervision meet a real need, but they can also be administered *en masse* to control aggressive behaviour in prison populations or undisciplined schools. Anti-depressants based on lithium, the world's mental stabilizer, are in wide use in the treatment of depressive illness, which absorbs a significant part of the health care budgets of western countries. But in parts of Texas the drinking water contains unusually high lithium levels and admissions to psychiatric hospitals are well below comparable levels elsewhere. So it has been seriously suggested that lithium should be added to drinking water in other cities as the best way of dealing with widespread depressive mental illness. Is it in principle different from mass fluoridation to control dental decay?

Not only the mentally ill, but those needing geriatric nursing, hyperactive and undisciplined children, violent and criminally active teenagers have all been cited as people in need of such treatment with or without their consent. It is conceivable that everyone could have their own, personal pill box, giving them the options of increased drive, creativity, optimism, or sexuality. Who is the real self when our behaviour can be managed in this way?

Brain stimulation can also be attempted by electrical means, in electro-convulsive therapy, for instance, which is used to treat certain mental conditions. Animal research has also shown that stimulation of appropriate parts of the brain can arouse aggression or make an animal more docile. And this form of stimulation has already been offered on an experimental basis to people with uncontrollably violent behaviour patterns. At the other end of the spectrum, but perhaps not wholly out of context, is the attractiveness to some people of the personal hi-fi. It is certainly mood manipulation, and allows the individual to withdraw to some extent from the reality around him or her. Just choose your cassette to arouse excitement, nostalgia, eroticism, or whatever mood you want.

In the reverse way, brain activity can be recorded electrically and analysed by computer. Abnormal activity can then be recognized and the information used. Epileptic fits, for example, can be pre-empted. We are now beginning to analyse our feelings before we actually feel them. While this particular use is obviously beneficial to the sufferer, the question must be answered, is there any facet of human beings that should not be subjected to analysis and control by technological methods?

Why the drive for control?

To make the system efficient

Most electrical and drug control techniques have been initiated with the benefit of the individual at least in mind. This is also true for the broadly educational aims of much reward-based conditioning. However, in the field of management science the aims of the whole exercise are very different. Our technological way of life has produced assembly-line factory production and the bureaucratic organization of society. These in turn need sophisticated management techniques to maintain them. Personality and individualism are sacrificed to the efficiency of the system.

Management techniques for the factory were developed to achieve maximum efficiency of machine production – maximum output. The guiding principles were, firstly, that any job should be broken down into a series of small, separate operations, each requiring a minimum of skill. Secondly, the process of planning the work should be completely removed from the process of doing it. Production workers were treated as extensions of the machines they operated. A rather extreme summing up of this management philosophy is given by Albury and Schwartz in their book *Partial Progress*. The quotation is taken from a journal of management science:

> 'We need an inventory of the manner in which human behaviour can be controlled. If this provides us with sufficient handles on human materials so that we can think of them as metal parts, electrical power or chemical reactions, then we have succeeded in placing human material on the same footing as any other material and can proceed with our problems of systems design.'

To solve problems quickly

This apparently irresistible dominance of technology over our lives is nowhere more obvious than in the growing use of computers as a management tool. Even areas of work previously thought to need a good deal of initiative and creativity on the part of the employee are being subordinated to the same, all-embracing technology.

Computer Aided Design (CAD), for example, is now widely used in engineering and architectural offices. It gives massive savings in time but has been seriously criticized for leading to deterioration in design quality.

It has been suggested that preliminary interviews with your friendly local bank manager and even with your GP or social worker could be conducted instead with a computer, as a more efficient way of obtaining routine information.

In this way, managers stand apart from the system whether it is a factory or the wider social community. They seek to reach conclusions about action without being part of the system or the cultural environment. Kenneth Galbraith, the American economist, sees this as the inevitable result of 'the technological imperative'.

To gain political and commercial power

Government

Technology is no longer primarily about tools to make life easier; it is about power struggles and control over every aspect of our lives. This is taking place in both the political and the commercial worlds. As we are learning from our news reports, the two are sometimes inextricable. Government-funded research into electronic surveillance techniques seems to have started a trend which cannot be stopped. Tabs are kept on an increasing number of our day-to-day concerns. Our welfare and health records, credit rating, tax returns and employment history are all recorded on centralized computer files. There are proposals to bring in universal finger-print and identification cards – computer readable of course. One criticism in the debate over the introduction of poll tax is that it involves a computer file identity check on all residents in an area. Scanning cameras with zoom lenses and the capacity to record all that they see can maintain a twenty-four hour watch on streets, stations, shops and banks. They are also being brought in to monitor football crowds, demonstrations and marches. Individual TV watching habits can be surveyed from mobile vans. Modern electronic telephone exchanges can store a record of calls made, and voice response equipment means that conversations which contain pre-selected key words can be recorded.

This is not fantasy; the equipment is already installed in workplaces and public buildings, and the ways in which it can be applied grow each year. The justification for these systems is sometimes hard to refute. They monitor costs, save time, help to maintain law and order, are 'just a new market research technique'. The problem is, once they have been seen to be effective in one situation, it is hard to resist using them in others. Such massive capacity for data collection and analysis is very impressive; it is easy to accept that it must somehow be needed. We are being more and more reduced to a managed society.

Big business

Big business is also vitally interested in a managed society. Most research topics funded by industry are designed to benefit turnover and profit rather than the consumer. The much acclaimed 'green revolution' was brought about by research which enabled new varieties of cereals to be produced – high yield varieties which would remove the threat of famine from the Third World. But such research was not entirely altruistic. These new cereal varieties needed large amounts of fertilizer and could only effectively be grown on mechanized farms. So, while large capital-intensive farms benefitted, the poor small-time farmers were excluded. At the same time the price of local food had to be raised so that all the investment in new machinery and fertilizers could be financed. The big industrial firms who launched the research benefitted from increased sales of fertilizers. Their market for pesticides also increased as the problems of monoculture became apparent. The local farmers are often no better off.

Why is it that the consumer, the individual at the bottom of the pile, gets such a hard deal? The reason lies partly in the assumption that, for every problem, there must be a technological solution – and, for a big problem, the solution must be big. Business organizations with the capacity to carry out research on this scale are only interested in markets of the hundred million pound size. Their research will inevitably be geared towards exploiting existing products while looking for new investment opportunities, and the real needs of people are easily ignored. This is just as true of our western society as it is for Third World agriculture. Very sophisticated information systems, for example, are available to us via our television screens. A large investment in research (which is ultimately paid for by the consumer) has given us access to computer files of data primarily of interest to managers of commercial and industrial businesses. Meanwhile I cannot buy a simple, cheap summary of all the TV programmes for the coming week! Whose interests are being served by those running the information industry? Why am I being managed in a way that is so obviously contrary to my simple needs?

Who is in charge?

In this massive transition to a post-industrial society, from a second-wave to a third-wave civilization, a choice is being made. This choice is between what has been called a 'soft' transition or a 'hard' transition. That is, between a system which gives more emphasis and opportunity to our non-material needs – our personality development and our individualism – or a system of hyper-organization which automatically assumes that large-scale, complex technology is the answer to our problems. The technology has already been given to us and is the product of our inventiveness. We are now making those choices about how it should be used.

These choices are very often made on the basis of greed, the urge to dominate, the quest for power. When the London Stock Exchange was in a turmoil of takeover fever during 1987, full-page advertisements told us that the death knell of one of our traditional industries was being sounded. Only if it became part of a giant corporation, able to take on the world, would it be able to survive in such a competitve market. All the products of the industry must be under centralized control, targetted to individual markets with competition removed. Product development would ensure the creation of new markets and react to international trends. Only in the strength of a multinational conglomerate could a prosperous future be assured, they said. You might easily assume they were talking about the aerospace industry or nuclear power, but you would be wrong. This was the publicity of Guinness Plc in support of their takeover of the Scotch Whisky industry. It is a long road indeed from the small family distilleries each making their own subtly characteristic product. The hard transition progressively does away with the craftsman and skilled worker, the self-employed and self-organized. People are thought of as a labour force to be phased out as soon as appropriate technology can be developed to replace them, and as a consumer market to be manipulated.

I have labelled our society 'aggressive' because I believe that, with a few exceptions, we see the human race as masters in a closed world. The basis of our thinking is reductionist: our analytical, scientific approach assumes that the whole is nothing but a collection of components, each of which can be studied in isolation. We are masters because our philosophy is dualistic: we see ourselves at the top of a pyramid with an inalienable right to exploit the whole of nature to satisfy our desires. As masters we have evolved a slave society built on machines but, as the history of other slave based civilizations has shown, there are hidden dangers in this way of life. In *Enemies of Society* Paul Johnson suggests that such a society has the seeds of decay built into its foundations, because the concept of freedom is so relative.Technicism is in fact making us the slaves of technology to the extent that our deep personal needs are of lower priority than the achievement of technological targets.

As *masters* in a closed world, we have no outside point of reference, no absolute standard by which we can judge our priorities. Michael Allaby, in a penetrating analysis in his book *Inventing Tomorrow*, has written that,

> 'For several centuries we have been pursuing a chimera. We are pursuing a quest for power that is robbing the planet of its physical materials. When they are gone the power will vanish. This pursuit of power has gone so far that the very life support systems of the planet are threatened. But the real mistake we have made is that our purpose has been to build paradise on earth and we have deluded ourselves. The problems are human ones of comprehension, communication, compassion and repentance. We have tried to solve them with mechanical excavators, nuclear power stations and oil refineries.'

Whose authority do we accept?

From a Christian point of view the situation just described can be summed up as a problem of authority. Just where, in contemporary society, do we turn to seek answers for the most important questions of life? Who or what do we accept as a final authority?

The overthrow of biblical authority

Man is always seeking to submit to some authority, not in the obvious sense of being under discipline but in his need to be able to justify his actions. It has been said that when man ceases to believe in God he doesn't believe in nothing, he believes in anything. So movement away from the conventional authority of the church has coincided with the spreading popularity of cults and the search for alternative mystical experience. Revolutions against traditional governments have denied that their authority is derived, however tenuously, from divine appointment. But this has led to the growth of secular totalitarian movements with the state having ultimate authority and being the final court of appeal.

The failure of science

Trust in divine providence for present needs and future hope has given way to an almost universal assumption that only science and technology can build a higher quality of life. The development of this belief can briefly be traced in the second half of the twentieth century. In the 1950s and 1960s science was widely assumed to hold the key to Utopia and the authority which justified this hope was the technical expertise and inventiveness of man.

In the 1970s this image of science became less convincing as some of the promised miracles failed. The green revolution did not solve the Third World famine problems, it only succeeded in expanding the market for the big multinational companies. Pesticides and antibiotics were by no means an unqualified success – resistant streams of insects and bacteria evolved faster than the chemists' products. The child prodigy of nuclear power failed to fulfil its early promises. The protest movements of the decade made their appeals on the basis of alternative authorities such as a responsibility to future generations, a need for careful stewardship of resources, our own long term self-interest and a concept of the world-wide brotherhood of man – an international egalitarianism. The concept of 'spaceship earth', a self-contained, self-sustaining capsule, became popular but the associated idea of a mission control station was forgotten. During the 1980s the massive failure of technology to deliver the fundamentals of a good life, as opposed to the incidentals, has become obvious. Massive unemployment in the technologically advanced countries, disastrous poverty in the Third World and new levels of international tension are so commonplace that we are learning to live with them.

Our technology seems unable to provide solutions to these problems. But more crucial than that is that the problems themselves are technology-led. Our machines are changing the nature of work faster than our social institutions can adapt. Our growing ability to control people as well as our environment has led to a new hunger and search for power.

The radical nature of these problems, that they are structural rather than superficial, does not seem to be appreciated. Rather, we reiterate our belief in expansion and economic growth. We appeal all the more desperately to the authority of technicism for the solution. Even the protest movements, valuable as they may be in challenging the assumptions, can only call for technology to be applied with a greater awareness of the side effects, a technology with a human face. They are hanging on, against all the evidence, to the hope of rescue by these means because they have nothing else and no one else to hang on to. If

God is rejected and his authority not recognized, then man can only turn to himself and to the idols he has created.

Alternative authorities

Man has always, it seems, preferred to submit to an authority other than the living God, but as we now look through examples from biblical history we shall see that all these authorities fail disastrously when used in isolation. Only if we use them under the supreme authority of the living God can their offers become at all realistic.

Even the Pharisees with all their 'religion' made this mistake. They were frequently in conflict with Jesus because he did not conform to their *tradition*. In Matthew 15:2, for instance, they complain to Jesus, 'Why do your disciples break the tradition of the elders? They don't wash their hands before they eat!' This tradition was held by some Jews to be an oral law given by God to Moses, but it was really just a humanly constructed set of rules which, Jesus said, they were manipulating for their own advantage. The Samaritans (John 4:20), were similarly bound by tradition, making it in effect a higher authority than God himself. We see Jesus cutting through this self-imposed authority to let the authority of God illuminate their lives.

Another very contemporary authority is that of *popular demand*, the guiding principle of democracy. But it is certainly not of modern origin. The demands of the Hebrew people led Aaron to make a visible, golden calf for them to worship instead of the invisible God (Exodus 32). Samuel gave way to popular demand to ask God for a king over Israel (1 Samuel 8). But in both cases the majority was wrong. The crowds of John 6:14–15, seeing the miraculous signs by Jesus, wanted to make him king, but he recognized that God's way was not the way of the popular vote. The popular vote is a fickle authority; mass opinion can be manipulated. The crowd who shouted 'Hosanna!' (Matthew 21:9), were probably very similar to those who shouted 'Crucify him!' (Matthew 27:22). The Kingdom of God is not a democracy.

Many people would rate *experience* as the highest guiding authority. Appeal to experience can clinch many an argument; seeing really *is* believing, most of the time. This was the criterion chosen by Thomas (John 20:25) and by Gideon (Judges 6:36–38); but it is an authority which can be misused, as we see in the case of the Pharisees in Matthew 16:1.

In a modern scientific age the self-evident *power of technology* and the system of logical thought behind it carry tremendous authority. In the story of Babel we find men trying to secure their future with the advanced technology of their time (Genesis 11:4). When David met Goliath he was equipped with the appropriate military hardware (1 Samuel 17:38–39), but fortunately he realized that it would be inappropriate for the occasion. The place where ultimate authority lies is pointed out very clearly by him: 'You come against me with sword and spear and javelin' (clearly a case of overkill, in modern jargon) 'but I come against you in the name of the Lord Almighty, the God of the armies of Israel, whom you have defied.' One of the penalties incurred by Israel in asking for a king was that they were then subjected to the full rigour of an organized technological system (see 1 Samuel 8:11; 1 Kings 10:14–29). Later it became clear that this diverted them from reliance on God as the only true and ultimate authority (see, for instance, Isaiah 31:1–3).

Satan tempted Jesus in the wilderness by the power of *logical thinking* (Matthew 4:1–10). His arguments have a modern ring about them. If God is loving why does he allow suffering? If God is all-powerful why does he permit evil? Jesus' answer was that God's authority cannot be judged by a man-made standard.

When the chief priests and elders challenged Jesus about the basis of his authority (Matthew 21:23), he showed them up as sitting on the fence, unwilling to commit themselves to a decision on whose authority they would recognize. On the one side, there was the authority of the professional expert, always open to disputed shades of meaning. On the other side there was God making absolute demands that were not negotiable. The great majority of people today are sitting on the same fence recognizing the authority of man in the ordering of their everyday lives, but unwilling finally to reject the possibility of God's higher authority.

Working under authority

We are often faced with the stark choice of having to jump to one side of the fence or the other; of having to submit ourselves to God's authority or to a man-made authority. But this is not always the choice set out in the Bible. We will look briefly at three men who were willing to recognize, and work with, secular authorities while at the same time bringing them all under the ultimate authority of God.

Nehemiah questioned those who had special knowledge of the conditions in Jerusalem, and accepted their reports. Then he used this information to make his prayers specific and relevant (Nehemiah 1:1–4). He then decided to ask the king for help and committed this decision to God for success (2:4–5). He was willing to use his own influence and position to obtain the authority of the king for the work God had entrusted to him. While busily engaged on rebuilding the walls there was a nice balance in the arrangements for ensuring that the work would be completed. 'We prayed to our God,' he says, 'and posted a guard day and night' (4:9).

Daniel's obedience to God directly conflicted with the demands of the Babylonian state. But he rose to high office in the court of Nebuchadnezzar, not by compromising his principles (Daniel 1:8), but by working sensitively within the system. There was, however, a sticking point at which the king's authority had to give way to a higher one (3:18).

God honoured Daniel's commitment and, through it, the king himself came to recognize and revere the supreme authority of God. It is important for us today to ask whether a similar stand can have similar results, or whether our society has gone past the point of no return and can no longer recognize the truth and authority of God even when brought to its notice.

In the New Testament we have an example of a time when Paul chose to work under human authority even when it conflicted with God's. On his voyage to Rome (Acts 27), Paul gave advice which conflicted with that of the experts, and he was overruled by a majority decision. It turned out to be a wrong decision and all seemed to be lost in a violent storm. But God promised Paul that although shipwreck was inevitable, the lives of all aboard would be saved. God does not choose to save us from the consequences of wrong decisions except insofar as his main purposes must be worked out. It is interesting that although Paul was assured that everyone would be saved he still felt impelled to take some direct action to retrieve the situation. Being under spiritual authority did not absolve him from looking ahead and taking practical, commonsense decisions (vs 31–34). But even in the emergency he gave thanks to God in front of everyone (v 35). So we see Paul submitting to both the political authority represented by the soldiers, and the technical authority represented by the sailors. Yet he was still able to bring good out of the disastrous situation they had got themselves into because the ultimate authority to which he was submitting was the authority of God. Perhaps one of the greatest missionary challenges for the twentieth-century church of the Western world is to demonstrate how the modern creed of technicism can be brought under the supreme authority of almighty God.

5

A machine-minded society

Our society has tunnel vision. It can focus clearly only on a very narrowly defined field of vision. We are so indoctrinated with the cult of the technological fix that we are less and less able to see that there may be alternative, less quantifiable solutions to some of our problems. We are caught up with the short term momentum generated by our industrial technology.

According to Schumacher we are living with three illusions: that infinite growth can take place in a finite environment; that there will always be an adequate supply of people willing to be machine slaves; and that science can solve all our problems. These three 'credal statements' form the foundation of a technological ideology. We make our decisions about changes in society on the basis of them. This leads to the mass institution, the international conglomerate, the assessment of every value in economic terms and the trivialization of so much of our lives.

Our society has developed in this way because of our powerful urge to explore and dominate our environment. Our amazing technology is the product of our inventive minds, as is the ideology of technical progress. But the time has come to see the dangers for which we are heading. We must widen our field of view from a tunnel to a full 360 degrees, and use our technology to liberate the potential of man, not to confine it. This is something which we will return to later on, but for the moment let us look at some examples of the effect which our machine-minded attitude is having on our lives.

Stand up for your rights!

We are surrounded by technological tools that are becoming more and more automated and fail-safe. We expect a machine to perform with one hundred per cent accuracy. The advertisements assure us that we can insure against the cost of a breakdown and, should a fault occur, a service engineer is on call.

We are beginning to expect one hundred per cent performance from our organizations. If the trains don't run on time or the gas bill is wrong then not only do we expect the fault to be corrected, there is also a sense of being let down; an uncomfortable feeling that this should not have happened. A machine-dominated society is insulating us from one of the raw facts of life, the existence of human error.

Mankind is now expected to reach ever higher standards of performance; our machine-dominated expectations have extended into our personal lives. We assume that our jobs, our health, our marriages should live up to our highest expectations. and when faults occur we expect instant service or part exchange! Paul Tournier writes in *The Gift of Feeling* about emotional solitude:

'Our society is anonymous and functional. Each of its members is defined not as a person but by his role. All that is demanded of him is that he fulfils his function, his intimate feelings do not count.'

Expecting all of life to function with mechanical precision has, I believe, led us on from anticipating benefits to demanding our rights. Economic growth, for instance, is no longer received as a blessing but is demanded as a right. Pressure groups call for the right to work, the right to a home, the right to choose, the right to happiness, the right to freedom. There are, of course, both good and bad aspects here. A call for freedom and rights has often been a necessary response to oppressive practices, motivated by a sense of responsibility to the under-privileged. This can still be true, but it seems that demands for rights can also alienate groups from each other. Pressure for ethnic minority rights can antagonize the rest of society and lead to more conflict instead of racial harmony. An emphasis on personal satisfaction distorts our understanding of what our deepest needs really are.

The cult of professionalism

Modern medicine has become a highly technological industry. A doctor, writing recently in a national newspaper, wrote of the impressive efficiency of modern techniques to destroy disease. But he contrasted this with their inadequacy in helping people come to terms personally with illness and death. He believed that the spectacular advances in techniques have conditioned doctors to see their main purpose as waging a relentless war on mortality. What is really needed, he said, is an improvement in the quality of life for those suffering from disease. Good medicine has always been holistic in its approach to the person, but increasing technological specialization and the desire to quantify results means in practice that doctors may leave the spirit to fend for itself.

An increasing emphasis on professionalism has also distorted our concept of personal responsibility. We become unsure of our ability to make sound decisions, even in the area of personal relationships. Instead, we shift the onus of decision-making on to 'experts', who are being asked to make judgments in areas outside their professional expertise. Take, for example, the right of doctors to prescribe contraceptives for girls under sixteen without parental consent. The House of Lords' judgment included this justification:

> 'To abandon the principle of doctor-patient confidentiality for children under sixteen might cause some not to seek professional advice at all. They could then be exposed to the immediate risks of pregnancy and sexually transmitted diseases as well as other long-term psychological and emotional consequences.'

We see here a confusion between specific technical advice on pregnancy and sexually transmitted disease, and the very much more personal relationships required to develop emotional maturity. It is assumed that a short-term, professional, doctor-patient relationship is as good for dealing with one problem as another. Expertise and authority in one field is being transferred to another to the detriment of long-term personal relationships and family responsibility.

Professional social services have done a tremendous amount to relieve the problems brought by industrial expansion but there is also a hidden cost that is not yet generally recognized. Professionalism in our caring services has produced a socially inept population. This is seen in a widespread reluctance to cope with day-to-day social problems within the family or local community – whether it is a matter of finding the money to live, clothing the children, or getting the grass cut. We have come to expect that an expert will be available who can sort it out for us. This is especially true in the anonymous life of major cities and suburbs where the isolation induced by our modern way of life is particularly acute. A Swedish youth council report says that their young people today are materially satiated and socially starved. How does a machine-minded society try to deal with its population's inability to cope? It points to material deprivation as the cause, and to the provision of more money and resources as the cure. All the human slot-machine needs to operate properly is the right coin.

It's measurement that matters

Every area of human activity and every social interaction is now subject to analysis, simulation techniques and attempts to predict and control behaviour. In the world of advertising, superlatives are piled on top of each other and have lost their power to impress. Even charity advertisements bombard us with statistics, the assumption being that anything on a large scale must be very important. Attempts to even prick our consciences must aim to overwhelm us. But why does it matter more if there are a million elderly people trying to cope alone than if there are only one hundred? What should matter to us is that there is *one* such person, in our street or in our family, for whom we are responsible. When problems are presented on such a large scale, however, there is a danger that many people will feel that only a correspondingly large-scale solution will do any good. This obviously must be the responsibility of governments, rather than individuals, and so simple personal caring becomes overtaken by an organized, institutional process.

Polls of public opinion are conducted on every

important current issue. Then the research departments of the political parties get to work on the results. They write up their manifestos, designing them as carefully as a new breakfast cereal to appeal to a chosen section of the consumer market. The values and ideals on which the electorate will vote are not those inspired by the vision of the leaders; they are thrown up instead from a statistical analysis of voting trends and returned questionnaires.

Modern commercial management techniques are geared only to profit and efficiency. Production units are shifted around the world, causing wholesale disruption of people's lives, in the quest for better profit ratios or yield factors. Ludicrous anomalies are produced by these attempts to make the managing of large-scale industries cost-effective. We can only shrug our shoulders helplessly as a subsidized agricultural system produces massive surpluses of butter, wine and beef, while other industries are closed down to avoid the production of surplus goods. We have come to accept, uncritically, that we must adapt to new technology at all costs, and that short-term economic gains are of overriding importance. Only what is measurable is considered important; only values that can be quantified are those that are reinforced.

A look-alike society

Finally, despite our unparalleled standard of living and our technical achievements, our culture is losing its diversity. This has been well charted in the ecological sphere where an industrially based agriculture is systematically destroying the habitat for wildlife at an alarming rate. In the supermarkets and retail stores we still appear to have considerable individual choice, but this is steadily being eroded. If the aim of production is to reach higher technical standards at a minimum cost, the products will inevitably begin to turn out looking very similar. Tight budgeting control of retail stocks eliminates slow moving lines, and cut-throat competition produces high street shops differing only in the gimmicks by which they try to sell their (almost identical) goods. Transport, entertainment, homes and gardens have all become submerged in the pre-packaged, look-alike society.

Why have we allowed, even welcomed, these machine-oriented aspects of life to dominate society? I believe it is because we have allowed the definition of our real needs to be grossly distorted. As a result, we are living with a totally wrong set of priorities. Schumacher suggests that we have three fundamental needs:

1. To act as spiritual beings.
2. To act as neighbourly beings.
3. To act as creative beings.

Our machine-minded society is making it increasingly difficult for most people to meet these needs – or even to realize that they have them. As a Church of Scotland minister, Campbell Campbell-Jack, wrote in the shadow of the nuclear technology of Dounreay,

> 'The world we shape becomes the reality to which we adjust. We do not merely shape society, we begin to remake ourselves in the image of the technology we have produced, adjusting our expectations, fears and hopes.' *(A Nuclear Babel? Third Way*, April 1986.)

God speaks to a machine-minded society

What is truth?

'What is truth?' is the question that Pilate asked Jesus, and philosophers have echoed it through the ages.

How do we find out the truth? Do we trust our senses? If we do we may find that what is true for me may not be true for you. So we end up with a rather large number of possible answers.

Do we follow our reason? This has been the answer most commonly given since the Renaissance, and it has reached its zenith of popularity in our own scientific era.

There is a third option: to seek revelation. As the popularity of the criteria of reason has increased, this option has become correspondingly less convincing, less respectable to logical, scientific man. Its current image is that of a rather quaint, religious anachronism. But the fact that we cannot quantify or measure the enigmatic claim of Jesus, 'I am the truth', should alert us to the fact that our machine-minded society has accepted too limited a view of truth. Today we are taught to accept as true only that which can be observed, repeated, and explained logically. Although most people would not realize it they judge events by what is called the scientific method. If we try to open a door with a key, but fail, we will very quickly analyse the various possibilities: we have the wrong key, the lock is jammed, or the door is bolted on the inside. We don't fear an evil spirit, or check the positions of the stars. We follow through the methods of experimental science, and we very quickly decide which of the three possibilities is correct. These methods are built on procedures involving collecting data, constructing an hypothesis to co-ordinate the data, devising a model to explain what is observed, using the model to predict future behaviour and testing the prediction experimentally.

We are so accustomed to working in this way in situations like that of the jammed door that we call it 'common sense', but it illustrates the authority which the methods of modern experimental science have come to have in our lives. Moreover, this is validated by the tremendous success that modern science has had in understanding and controlling the natural world. Respect for this authority is built into our education system, is exploited in the commercial and industrial world, and pervades our social and political life.

Can God be pushed out?

If we accept the scientific method as the only basis for understanding truth, the only way in which we can search for meaning, then we are restricting ourselves within a man-centred framework to what can be imagined, measured and repeated.

Extracts from John Gribben's book *In Search of the Big Bang*, published in *The Guardian* newspaper, describe how scientists are constructing theories about the first moments of creation of the physical world. He makes this claim:

> 'One fact of overriding importance is clear. The human laws of physics operating in accordance with the observed behaviour of the universe on the largest and smallest scales are alone sufficient to explain how everything came into being, spontaneously, at a definite moment of creation about fifteen thousand million years ago. The ultimate question of physics has indeed been answered. Is there then still a role for God?'

This quotation is typical of the general attitude to science that comes across on television, in our newspapers and in much of the educational material used in schools. In it there are two fundamental mistakes. The first is the assumption that once a natural process is accounted for and understood man is somehow in control of it. Before a workable theory of creation was devised, 'God' was convenient to use as an explanation for those events which man could not understand. But with the progress of science he has become dispensible. This has been called a 'God of the gaps' theology and is obviously committed to the diminishing importance and final extinction of God as scientific knowledge develops. This God of the gaps is not the God who reveals himself to us in the Bible, where we are told he not only created but also sustains all things by his powerful word (Hebrews 1:2–3). The God presented by the Bible is continuously active in his world, in technology and industry, in family and community life, and in international relationships. As we shall see in Chapter 7 he is a covenant God, overruling the whole creation, not just the gaps in our knowledge of it.

Is scientific knowledge complete knowledge?

The second mistake is the idea that when our scientific knowledge is sufficiently developed it is able to offer a *complete* explanation of reality. The assumption here is that if and when quantum physics is able to explain the whole of a physical process then that process is nothing but quantum physics. This philosophical assumption has been called by Donald Mackay, 'nothing buttery'. It implies the acceptance, as an act of faith, that the whole of reality is limited to what is measurable and comprehensible in our four-dimensional space-time world. Reality is defined by the limits of man's imagination and power of reasoning. There is no room for mystery, no concept of the transcendent.

Such self-imposed limitations in our understanding of reality do not only arise out of our scientific culture. The Pharisees made a very similar error. They had their law, a complicated set of rules governing behaviour in every circumstance of life, a total system for living. It was man-made, measurable, repeatable. Jesus accused them of hypocrisy (Mark 7:6–8) because they were taking a partial model of reality and acting it out as if it were the whole of reality. Their religion was nothing but external rules and regulations to the exclusion of inner thoughts and motives. It had become such a watertight system that there was no room for God to act in it, no role for him except as a nominal figurehead. On another occasion we get right to the heart of the matter. In John 5:39 Jesus showed that the Pharisees' concept of truth was too limited. They regarded the scriptures, the Old Testament, as being a revelation of God and they worshipped the words. They had forgotten that their covenant God is one who acts and that the Bible is only the record of him revealing himself. So, because of their preconceived ideas of what could be true, they actually met with Jesus face to face and did not realize that God was revealing himself to them.

Christians today can sometimes try to serve God within a self-imposed set of rules. It may be that their active service for God is limited by ideas of what activities are 'spiritual' and what are 'secular'. All of us need to be challenged over whether or not we suffer from tunnel vision.

Spiritual blindness

H G Wells, in his short story *The Country of the Blind*, tells of a remote community, cut off for generations from any contact with the rest of the world. They have a well-organized economic and social life but, due to an inherited genetic defect, they are all completely blind. As a result they are totally unable to understand concepts which involve sight. Shreds of belief and tradition surviving from an era before their blindness are dismissed by their wise men as idle fancies, now replaced with modern, rational explanations. They construct their own self-consistent model of reality – of the natural world – partly derived from their senses and completed by hypotheses built largely on faith. Into this closed world comes a sighted man. He is quite unable to communicate what he means by being able to see. The climax comes when the elders decide that this visitor has a physical defect, a deformity in his face which is producing severe brain damage. The remedy is obvious to them: surgically remove the deformity and he will be cured.

In Western technological society we are in danger of becoming a country of the blind, of closing our minds to the possibility of an extra dimension to reality that cannot be reached through our physical senses. As James Houston says in *I Believe in the Creator*, 'The landscape of the mind projects upon the landscape that we see.' We are putting limits on our vision of reality because we are accepting the ethos of a machine-minded society.

Is coherence the same as truth?

Another error we have made is to confuse coherence with truth. This is a problem that appears in many different forms, some more important than others. In *The Lord of the Rings*, J R R Tolkien constructs an imaginary world which is so convincing that we live alongside the characters in a way that can be totally absorbing. All the small details of their lives interlock in a coherent pattern but, though engrossed, we never confuse this with truth even if the story can show us something of what is true. The same could be said of *The Archers* on BBC Radio and of the best of television soap opera.

Science has been so persuasive over the last few years because it is beginning to provide a coherent description of the physical world. It includes in its scope not only the immensity of the universe and the incredibly small nuclear building blocks of matter, but also the intricate biological systems that we are ourselves. There are no longer any gaps in our experience; science has penetrated everything. As Christians we must learn to come to terms with this and to seek to understand more of what it means. We must see that God is the Lord of all creation including our technological expertise.

It is important to realize that any understanding we have is only partial. It is a selective view of truth. If we see it as the whole truth, we get a distorted picture of reality. For instance, we accept maps as an accurate description of the physical world. They are so comprehensive that it is sometimes difficult to remember that they present only a partial view of truth. The familiar map of the world based on Mercator's projection has been the basis of children's geography for generations and they have grown up believing that England was about one quarter the size of India. The very process of reducing reality to an easy-to-understand presentation leads to distortion. Similarly we are shown a selective scientific picture of how something works and we tend to go along unquestioningly with the implication that the world it represents is mechanistic and impersonal.

Even in the sheltered confines of most Christian experience we can fall into the trap of wearing blinkers that narrow our vision. Denominationalism or fundamentalism can be systems of belief which give us only partial views of reality. Liberation theology or the gift of healing, if combined with the implication that other experiences of God are of secondary importance, can be dangerous misunderstandings of the truth.

The Sadducees were caught in the same way, blinded by their own distortions of the truth from seeing what had already been revealed to them about resurrection from the dead (Matthew 22:23–32). Biblical teaching lifts our vision beyond the realm of the physical world. It transports us from the standpoint of the human observer to that of a larger, eternal perspective where, as it were, God lifts the veil and allows us to glimpse a deeper reality. The psalmist sets man in his true place in the world, less than God but steward of the earth (Psalm 8). In Psalm 139 he also shows how we are inescapably involved in a spiritual dimension to life, whether we like it or not:

'O Lord, you have searched me
  and you know me.
You know when I sit and when I rise;
  you perceive my thoughts from afar . . .
All the days ordained for me
  were written in your book
  before one of them came to be.

(vs 1–2, 16)

Isaiah tries to raise our sights to an infinite horizon (Isaiah 40:18–28) and shows us how transient and insignificant are our endeavours:

'To whom, then, will you compare God? . . .
He brings princes to naught
  and reduces the rulers of the world to nothing.
No sooner are they planted,
  no sooner are they sown,
  no sooner do they take root in the ground,
than he blows on them and they wither.'

In Job 28 our scientific knowledge is seen in relation to a greater awareness of a truth that we cannot totally comprehend. The writer of Job acknowledges man's technical ingenuity, his industry, his adventurous exploration, his uniqueness in creation. But, the author says, man is so dazzled by his discoveries that he has lost his ability to recognize true wisdom and understanding. He cannot measure it and put a price on it so he does not value it highly. He is so technically oriented that he no longer knows the fear of the Lord. Job 28:1–2, 9–13 reads:

'There is a mine for silver
  and a place where gold is refined.
Iron is taken from the earth,
  and copper is smelted from ore . . .
Man's hand assaults the flinty rock
  and lays bare the roots of the mountains.
He tunnels through the rock;
  his eyes see all its treasures.
He searches the sources of the rivers
  and brings hidden things to light.
But where can wisdom be found?
  Where does understanding dwell?
Man does not comprehend its worth;
  it cannot be found in the land of the living.'

6

A double-glazed society

An unending stream of unsolicited mail and persuasive telephone calls bombards us with offers to insulate our homes to a higher degree of comfort than ever before. With new materials and techniques we can cut the heat loss to a minimum, stop the draughts and shut out the traffic noise. We can even choose coated glass to give us extra privacy.

As a technological society, we are erecting double glazing between ourselves and a large part of reality, including other people. The benefits of a high standard of living have dulled our spiritual awareness, and the technological infrastructures on which we have come to depend filter out some of the essential ingredients of being human. Mankind has become alienated from his neighbour and from the rest of creation.

Let us now look at some of the facts of society which

are contributing to what I have termed the 'double glazing' effect.

The dreaming suburb

The drift to the suburbs has been a feature of life in Western society for the last fifty years. It is a logical development of a mass industrial and mass media society. The car, television, automatic washing machine, telephone and credit card seem to reduce the need for dependent social contact. We can now live unprecedentedly private lives with the aid of our socially isolating appliances.

A potted history of one domestic technology illustrates the point. Centuries ago in isolated village communities the family washing was done at the well or by the river bank. It was slow and inefficient, but no doubt a fertile scene for local gossip; people's ears would have itched for miles around. With the growth of a more affluent and urban society hot water became readily available at the public baths. This soon gave way to hot and cold on tap in the home. The family wash was still hung out in the garden in between chat over the garden fence. Then the washing machine thankfully took the hard labour out of the process and the launderette replaced the river bank, but now the final stage is upon us. In the suburbs the built-in tumble drier means that we now complete the family wash without leaving the house. The only contact with other people is the service engineer's annual visit.

Surely we can set our unparalled communications systems against the losses caused by this sort of change? We may not catch up on the relatives' news in person, but we can phone them. Telephones and easy travel are not, however, net gains in the communications stakes. They can only partly compensate for the isolation technological development has already produced. Similarly, television is not purely an opportunity to stimulate our imagination and enrich our lives. It has become little more than a method of mass sedation, a way of passing the time for a society which has lost the community structures which would enable its members to live fulfilled lives in relationships with other people.

Martin Pawley, writing of what he calls *The Private Future*, claims that Western society is on the brink of collapse into withdrawal. The media catalogue the collapse of the old system of community values and obligations, but do not give any real answers to the problems that result. This is because the process of collapse is always seen as a disease for which we seek a cure. Pawley claims that it is never seen for what it really is, a voluntary act of withdrawal by people who have chosen to accept the benefits of modern technology without seriously counting the cost.

Suburban life is the evasion of public encounter. It is designed for private rather than public transport. Sophisticated video and hi-fi provide private entertainment, and hypermarket shopping supplies our basic needs as impersonally as possible. The cost is borne in depleted village and inner city communities, and in the fast disappearance of the small, independent shopkeeper and the local cinema and theatre. The city, suburb, neighbourhood and street no longer form community units. The only corporate identity we have now is a freemasonry of private ownership. This has nothing to do with belonging, everything to do with receiving.

Secondary reality

Pawley coins a term to describe this situation. He calls it 'secondary reality'. By this he means that we have deliberately deceived ourselves about the nature of events in order to survive in our technological lifestyle. Secondary reality is promoted by government and industry, disseminated by the willing media and accepted uncritically by the majority of the population. In effect, it means that we live with the realities of one world by pretending that we live in another.

For example, considerable research, combined with government propaganda and legal penalties, do very little to reduce the toll of road accidents from alcohol abuse. Similarly the risks involved in cigarette smoking continue to be ignored by very many people. The secondary reality constructed by the advertising world encourages us to ignore the facts in favour of an illusory private satisfaction. Government action is cautious and moderate, taking care not to offend major interests. No manufacturer dares to advertise – or even admit – that alcoholic drinks on sale can make you drunk. No government has dared to raise taxes on cigarettes so much that sales are really reduced. We are content to make and accept token gestures of disapproval. Real public concern remains muted and ineffective because we are prepared to accept a (considerable) degree of suffering and injustice in order to enjoy the benefits of these products.

In a sense, entertainment has always provided an opportunity for us to participate in secondary reality. The travelling fair and theatre, and folksongs around the fire were in part a means of escape from the harshness of real life. But they were also a community experience in which the real hopes and fears of people could be expressed. With the mass move to the city the music halls attempted to carry on this tradition, and were gradually developed into an entertainment industry. Today television pipes in mass-produced entertainment to almost every home in the western world. It is a major commercial enterprise with immense profits to be made, and its influence on public attitudes is extraordinarily powerful. But it does not present us with objective, unbiased reporting of national and world news, nor does it offer us a reasonably wide choice of entertainment. Instead, because of political and economic pressures, it packages fragments of reality and edits them skilfully into an acceptable, second-hand product. We see edited, time-shifted, mood-creating sequences of images which are designed primarily to hold an audience rather than to convey information or stimulate thinking.

Because television must retain its audience from one week to the next every question must remain open. The commentator must always have a future entrance, there must always be an alternative view. So television suspends its judgement and invites us to do the same. Its influence lies in its ability to distract rather than analyse, and to maintain a continuous level of excitement. Whether it is in the contest quiz show with ever more glittering prizes or the *Tomorrow's World* type of science reporting, we are encouraged to live in a dream world of ever greater affluence, more powerful technology, more effective pills. Even in the relaying of snooker tournaments the tension is maintained at an artificial high by skilful editing. It requires concentrated effort to realize that we rarely see any of this live, our match is really constructed in the tape cutting room!

Similarly in politics our leaders and personalities come to us neatly packaged, their scripts written for them and well-rehearsed in every detail. The main issues of a political programme are chosen to appeal to the voter, like next year's fashions. Both the politicians and the voters know what is going on. And yet we prefer to cover the reality with a glossy veneer, a facade of involvement. This veneer covers a general desire to be left alone, bribed and pacified by promises of increasing affluence.

The technology of today enables us to opt out of public life into an artificial private world. People and products are marketed in the dream world of secondary reality but we all have to live and work in a world of primary reality. Disappointment is inevitable – compare your experience of car driving with the image presented by the advertisements! The industrial state exists by promoting a dream world but it cannot deliver what it promises. We wait optimistically for a final technological solution to our problems – better housing, new pills, cheap energy, the age of leisure – but when individuals realise they are not, in fact, going to get these things, they react with apathy, cynicism, disorder and violence. Furthermore, by looking to technology to solve all our problems we continue to destroy the community aspects of society which make it stable and interdependent. We are losing the ability to share our hopes, fears and suffering with others. Television instead has become the companion of the lonely, drugs the nirvana of the desperate; and the social services attempt desperately to meet what they think is mainly an economic need.

A hard case

This double-glazed world reduces our ability to respond to a spiritual initiative from God. But the situation is not unique.

In the Bible we come across quite a few instances which show this happening. One of the best known is Pharaoh, confronted with the demands of Moses to let the Israelites go out from Egypt (Exodus 4:21, 7:3–4, 14:4). In Exodus 8:15 we see it stated that Pharaoh 'hardened his heart' against the request. Why? Because he was ifluenced by his magicians who could apparently do similar things to Moses and because the immediate crisis had passed. There was no longer any *need* to obey a God who he did not think was all-powerful, when he, Pharaoh, was still in control. Pharaoh, isolated from a greater reality by the trappings of his own power, could not conceive of someone greater than himself breaking in from outside.

The way in which this is expressed can cause difficulty because it appears that God is saying *he* has hardened

Pharaoh's heart as if Pharaoh himself had no option in the matter. But this would be contrary to the clear and consistent message throughout the Bible that God gives people a choice in their relationship with himself and holds them responsible for their own actions. God has *preknowledge* of all that happens. In Exodus 3:19 he warned Moses that Pharaoh's heart would be hardened against him.

Such foreknowledge does not take away our responsibility for the choices we make. This kind of knowledge is often there, in an imperfect way, in our own lives. It is similar to the way we ourselves are certain about some of the choices that our intimate friends will make, because we appreciate the pressures they are working under and know the way they tend to react. We think we know, in advance, what they will choose, and very often we are right. How much more does God know our inner motivations!

The Egyptian army in pursuit of the Israelites was motivated by a similar blindness to that of Pharaoh (Exodus 14:17, 21–23). In spite of all the evidence of the plagues, the killings of the first-born, the exodus from Egypt and the waters of the sea receding, it still pressed on blindly, thinking that might was right.

Much later on in Israel's history we find Daniel in the court of Nebuchadnezzar. He is portrayed as a king so corrupted by his absolute power that, in his arrogance and pride, he is almost incapable of understanding what God says to him through Daniel.

Daniel interpreted a dream for Nebuchednezzar which threatened judgement, and summed it up with:

> 'Therefore, O king, be pleased to accept my advice. Renounce your sins by doing what is right, and your wickedness by being kind to the oppressed. It may be that then your prosperity will continue.'

Though desperately frightened at the time by the dream, we find the king twelve months later unrepentant:

> ' . . . as the King was walking on the roof of the royal palace of Babylon, he said, "Is not this the great Babylon I have built as the royal residence, by my mighty power and for the glory of my majesty?" ' (Daniel 4:27–30).

God finally brought him to humble himself and submit to a power infinitely greater than himself and his kingdom. The cost to him in personal suffering was, however, very great.

Belshazzar, Nebuchadnezzar's successor, seems to have completely ignored all the evidence he grew up with of God's power over Babylon. He insulated himself from the reality of which this spoke, until it broke in upon him in judgement and overwhelming power (Daniel 5).

In the New Testament we are told that even the disciples had hardened hearts. In Mark 6:52, after they had seen the multitude fed, they still did not seem to recognize Jesus for who he was. In Mark 8:17 there is a similar situation. We can hardly believe that the disciples were hardened in the same way as Pharaoh or Belshazzar, but Jesus accused them of having something in common. They had eyes to see and ears to hear, but failed to perceive the presence of God. The common factor was a wrong set of preconceived ideas, an insulating layer or a sort of double glazing between themselves and spiritual realities. Paul writes of this when he talks of the Jews having a veil covering their hearts (2 Corinthians 3:15).

What was this insulation? In a large part it was made up of the culture in which they lived and the teaching they had received from their leaders. Jesus told them to 'beware' of the Pharisees and the Herodians. That is, he warned them of the Pharisees' corrupted teaching, and of their religious élitism which set up a divide between the world and their concept of spiritual reality. On the other hand, Jesus was also warning against a too easy acceptance of the ruling Roman culture with its materialistic values. The call to God's people is to walk a spiritual tight-rope, to be in the world but not of it, to be salt and light in a world that has almost lost its sense of need. If we fail in this mission we may actually be responsible for people missing out on a meeting with God.

Lastly, in the New Testament the accusation of a hardened heart is levelled at the whole of society. In Matthew 13:10–15 and the parallel passage in Mark 4:9–12 Jesus explains that the crowds cannot understand his parables because they have closed their eyes to what he is really doing and stopped listening to what he is actually saying. They have made themselves almost incapable of response to a spiritual initiative. Many of Jesus' conversations with the Pharisees and Sadducees confirm this (see, for instance Matthew 12:38–42, and 16:1–4). On the other hand, even the slightest hint of the presence of God is picked up by those who are looking for him (Matthew 13:11, 16). Paul takes up the same theme in Romans 1:18–23. God does not hide himself from us but, by choosing to ignore him, we have made ourselves unable to recognize him.

We face the same temptations and dangers today. We see the comfortable society we have made for ourselves and we believe it will always stay that way. We are so excited with our ability to manipulate the world that we have forgotten who sustains it by his power. With our minds shaped by technicism we see only secondary reality; we have limited the size of our world and do not allow God into it.

PART THREE

God's claim on a technological society

7

Creation and covenant

So far we have been looking at various aspects of modern society with the aim of showing how they fit into a pattern. It is like a jigsaw puzzle with only a few of the pieces in place. The picture being formed is of a society undergoing a dramatic and rapid transformation because of the influence of technological attitudes.

Of course the picture is a biased one. The jigsaw pieces have been chosen because we have been looking for a particular kind of evidence, we have a hypothesis for which we seek confirmation. But this jigsaw is two-sided; if we turn it over we see the incalculable benefits we enjoy from our technological developments. Our lives have an amazing richness, variety and freedom because of the privileged times in which we live, and very few people would suggest that we should try to retrace the steps that have led us to this position. But without in any way discounting the credit side of our technological achievement it is crucially important to assess from a specifically Christian point of view what lies on the debit side.

Reactions against some of the more obvious ill effects of technology are already well known. The ecology movement and the anti-nuclear, motorway and pollution lobbies receive good publicity. The sane core of these movements fulfils a very important role in moderating some of the more extreme technological dreams of the planners. Others, notably some writers, have attempted to look into the future, and their views of our prospects range from the extremely pessimistic to the very optimistic. Their views are personal and their appeal is to human authority and humanly justified values. In this way they are working within the confines of our double-glazed society. In contrast, the base line of this book is a belief that there is an absolute authority and a given set of values to live by, independent of our personal preferences and cultural situation. Our critique of modern technological society is therefore based on the assumption that there is a God-given prescription for the best way of life.

Biblical guidelines for the use of technology

There is very little in the Bible to guide us directly to a theology of technology. There is nothing at all about nuclear power or computers and no easy guidance on ethical issues raised by modern medicine. But there is a very great deal about relationships between people in the light of their relationship with God; it is from this that we shall try to establish some guidelines for the way in which we should be using our technological skills.

Relationships

Firstly, our relationship to God has been affected by our rejection of him. Our scientific attitude continues the process of alienation by suppressing our sense of transcendence. Many people are reluctant to admit any place for mystery in their lives. More importantly our ability to give scientific explanations for much of what goes on in the world is leading us to deny the possibility that a God could be at work in it. This is in direct conflict with the biblical revelation of a creating God, who became incarnate in Jesus Christ.

Secondly, our relationships with each other are affected, becoming merely instrumental. Jacques Ellul claims that natural relationships between people are being replaced by 'technological' relationships. We are labelled by what we do rather than who we are. Because our relationship with God is severed we are losing the concept of the image of God in man. There is then no fundamental bond between us; we simply use each other, like tools, to satisfy our wants and needs.

Thirdly, our relationship with the material world is affected. We live in close interdependence with the material world and yet we assume that we have an inalienable right to exploit it. We have lost sight of the biblical idea of stewardship, of holding nature as a gift on trust from God. We have assumed instead the role of master, putting ourselves firmly at the top of a pyramid model of nature.

These broken and distorted relationships are not unique to the twentieth century. Biblical history is full of examples of people turning their backs on God and reaping the consequences in their relationships with others and society as a whole.

The creation mandate

The first three chapters of Genesis give us the foundations for the whole history of mankind, and the basic principles from which everything else develops. So this is where we must start in our study of the relationships between God, mankind, and the material world. We can show these relationships in a diagram:

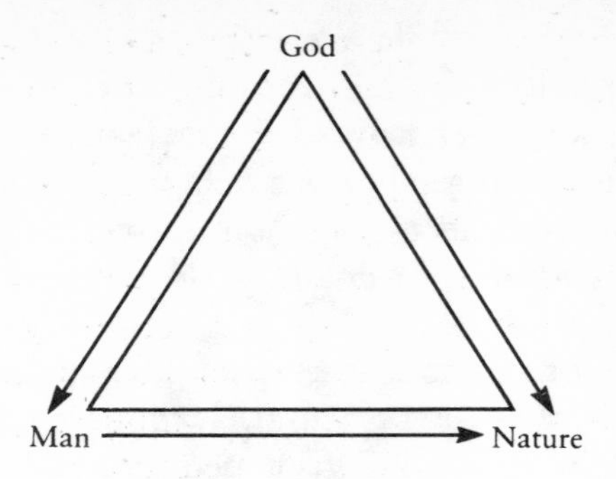

God is at the top of the triangle, the Lord of creation. In the beginning there was God. Creation took place at his word. He said 'let there be', and there was. In a few simple verses we see the completeness of this creation, the finished work of God the master craftsman.

But there are also some details which need to be registered. While mankind is an integral part of God's creation, formed from the dust of the ground, there is also a clear distinction between mankind and nature. Mankind received a special gift: the breath of life, direct from God (Genesis 2:7). He is given freedom of choice, responsibility for the care of creation, and the capacity to suffer for wrong decisions (Genesis 2:15–17). He is made in the image of God and thus has a unique relationship with him. Man is given authority to name all the living creatures. Throughout the Bible the giving of names is symbolic. To know the name of a person is to know their essential character and have power over them. So we see God appointing man as his steward over nature, to take part in the work of creation.

The world of nature is the stage for a meeting point between mankind and God. There has always been a temptation to idealize unspoilt natural places as the only places where God can be met, or of going one stage further and regarding the natural world itself as sacred. This is not what is being stated here. Rather, the picture of Genesis chapters 1 and 2 is one of God's involvement with the created world, of mankind's communication with him and of the created world being entrusted to mankind for his responsible use (Genesis 1:28–30).

What was established was a network of responsibility and protection. God had undertaken to care for mankind and for the created world; mankind would share in this work and live in a harmonious relationship both with God and with the created world. The created world, wisely governed by man, would supply his needs and provide a hospitable environment for him.

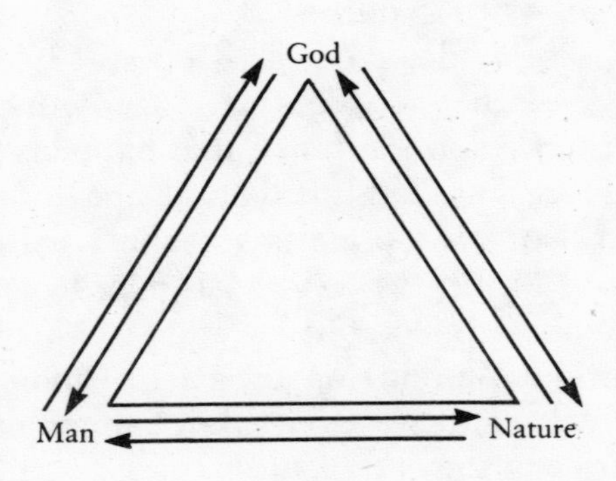

A fallen world

When man misused the freedom God had given him, the relationships which provided the structure for a stable world broke down. Man tried to sever the relationship with God in order to become autonomous (Genesis 3:5 and 3:10). The effect of that sin spread out, also affecting the bond between nature and God (Genesis 3:17, 18). It no longer reflects God's character as it once did (Genesis 1:31). Man's relationship to nature also changed, becoming antagonistic. The peace or shalom which had pervaded the whole design was lost because these relationships were broken.

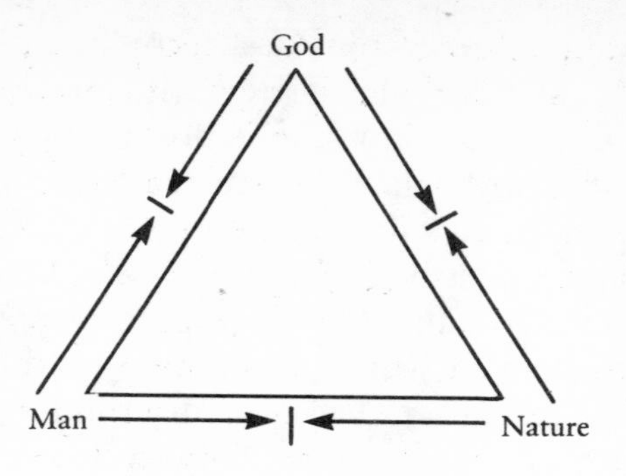

The covenant with Noah

The fallen world depicted in Genesis 3 deteriorates dramatically as the consequences are worked out in succeeding chapters. But nothing that happens can change the supreme fact that God is still at the apex of the triangle and in control of events. He is still the Lord of creation and is Lord of history as well. Man may have attempted to sever the link with God but the story of Noah illustrates that a 'go it alone' policy on the part of man is not one which God will endorse – yet. Man cannot live without God; if he tries to the end result is total destruction, both of himself and of the created order.

The deluge and its results are an almost total reversal of the creation process. When it is all over, the world is virtually back to the condition it was in at Genesis 1:1. In a situation that has parallels with that of creation, God re-establishes the creation mandate (Genesis 9:1–7); the words used are very reminiscent of Genesis 1:28–31. The role of Noah is very much like that of Adam. In Noah, man's delegated power over nature is restated, responsible stewardship is called for and the inevitable penalties for abusing a God-given freedom are spelt out.

But there is one vital difference: Noah is to exercise his stewardship in a *fallen* world. The triangular relationship is not as it should be, and God recognizes this changed situation by making laws designed to preserve life in a world where it is now constantly under threat.

God speaks to Noah of his covenant. Generally in the Old Testament a covenant is a formal declaration of the basis of a relationship. Two people or groups of people are involved. On the one hand there is the giver who promises certain benefits and, on the other hand, there is the receiver who has to fulfil certain conditions. It is based on mutual trust and responsibility and involves special personal obligations and privileges.

As with most covenants, the covenant with Noah does not actually bring into being a relationship, but rather affirms a relationship which already exists. God confirms this with the *whole* of mankind, through Noah who stands as their representative, and also with the whole of creation. Only an infinite and eternal God could invest meaning into such a covenant; there are no obligations which either mankind or the created world can fulfil in order to sustain it. The relationship of protection and lordship is one which God will maintain.

The covenant is most significant though, because of its long-term aim. The flood was a demonstration of God's right to wipe out from the earth all who sin against him, but his provision of a way of escape for Noah, and his subsequent words to him show that total destruction was not the option he would take. Instead, God extends his grace to mankind, with the ultimate aim of restoring total harmony to the world. He will use the time of grace to bring about the reconciliation of man both to himself and to the created world. In this respect the covenant differs from others. There is nothing man has to do to ensure that this covenant of grace continues. God takes it upon himself to extend it unconditionally until the end of the world.

During this time, although there will not be complete restoration of the relationships on the triangle, the potential for their restoration is there, and can be partially realized:

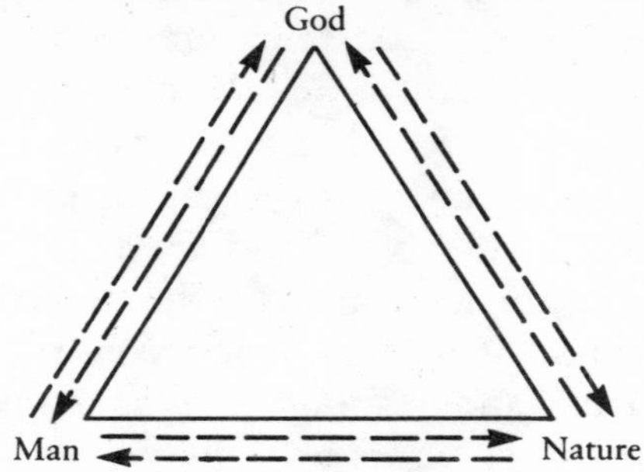

For us today this means that our position of trust and responsibility under God still holds. But it also means that our attempts to restore harmony to the world will not work unless at the same time we are being reconciled to God. This is where the Bible's covenant teaching becomes more specific.

Science has given us the ability to explain and control much of the natural world. But our understanding of the *mechanisms* of nature does not challenge the biblical message of God's ultimate *purpose* for the whole of creation.

The covenant with Israel

> ' "You yourselves have seen what I did to Egypt, and how I carried you on eagles' wings and brought you to myself. Now if you obey me fully and keep my covenant, then out of all nations you will be my treasured possession. Although the whole earth is mine, you will be for me a kingdom of priests and a holy nation." These are the words you are to speak to the Israelites.' (Exodus 19:4–6).

God's special covenant with the nation of Israel made at the giving of the law of Sinai, and the working out of its consequences through history, is a major theme of the Old

Testament. In the chapters following its introduction we see the sort of behaviour that God expected from them, and are repeatedly reminded that his faithfulness and love will be theirs in return. The Israelites were, for example, warned against oppressing foreigners and the defenceless, because this would anger God (Exodus 22:21–24). They were not to be exploitative because God is compassionate. They were to be just because God is just (Exodus 23:6) and they were to observe sabbaths as a reminder that God is holy (Exodus 31:13). We are also given some pictures to illustrate this covenant relationship. It is like the relationship between a mother and her child or between a man and his wife. It is a very special partnership in which God chooses to involve man in his creative work.

We are also told why God chose to make this covenant so specific to Israel. They were offered a special privilege and a special responsibility. They were to show something of God's holiness to the world and through them the nations of the world were to be reconciled to him. In this way the broken relationships between God, man and creation would ultimately be restored.

Although starting life as a nation under God with such high ideals it very quickly became apparent that Israel was not going to be able to live up to them. They distanced themselves from God to such an extent that as a nation they were no longer guided by covenant principles. So they failed in their role as witnesses of God's grace to the world.

A new covenant

Even as the prophets charted the reasons for the fall of Israel they were also looking forward to God's plan for a new covenant. Its mediator would not fail in his task of reconciling people to God.

The new covenant is made between God and individuals who are willing to accept a direct relationship with him through Jesus Christ. This is God's final demonstration of his covenant to man. In Jesus Christ he has personally come down the sides of the triangle and become physically involved in his creation. Thus God makes a very specific and very personal challenge to all people to accept the complete lordship of Christ and, through him, to enter into a covenant relationship with God.

Those who accept this challenge inherit both the privileges and responsibilities of Israel. As citizens of the kingdom of God the role of every Christian is to bring God's holiness and love into a world which has broken its relationship with him.

The basis of Christian action today

Those who have accepted Jesus Christ as Saviour and Lord are, by definition, his covenant people. What does this imply about our lifestyle and our relationships in the world? Paul says that we live as aliens in a foreign land. We differ fundamentally from the society around us on issues such as our ultimate source of authority, the concept of truth and the recognition of sin as rebellion against God. Most people today assume that society will gradually improve, provided that we can get the social programming right, the economy expanding and an improved political communication system. But we are also seeing a deep conflict between the struggle for rights and the desire for freedom. When there is no submission by common consent to an over-ruling authority these two ideals will always be in conflict. The covenant balance of freedom with responsibility, and its concept of freedom within the limits of God's law, are not considered relevant in contemporary society. Perhaps as Christians we are failing to present the challenge of working under the authority of almighty God in our daily lives. We need to demonstrate covenant relationships in practice.

Before we look at some possible lines of action, it will

be good to remind ourselves of Jesus' teaching on the working out of the new covenant ethic. He does not give us detailed rules for action. Rather he takes us behind the actions themselves and challenges us with the much more fundamental question of motivation. In other words, he repeatedly makes us look at the man-God and God-man link of the triangle in order that we correctly relate in the man-nature and nature-man area of life.

He poses a number of questions. Are we, at least in part, using other people as a means of boosting our own self-image (Matthew 6:1–16)? Do we base our lifestyle on a humanly constructed set of values or is our foundation absolute, God-given? John tells us that we face strong pressure to seek praise from men more than praise from God (John 12:43). Jesus faces us with a clear choice between the shallow commitment to a religious idea and a total assent to the obligations of the covenant he offers with the living God.

Our thinking is as important as our actions (Matthew 5:21–22, 5:27–28; Mark 7:14–23). For if our thinking has a wrong bias it will transfer to our lifestyle. This was the main thrust of Jesus' criticism of the Pharisees (Matthew 23). They were sheltering behind an institution instead of getting involved in covenant responsibilities (Matthew 23:23–26; Mark 7:1–13). They were suffering from tunnel vision. They had some of the characteristics of our machine-minded society, because a humanly constructed system of values was determining their priorities for living. The commandments not only set a standard for our behaviour but also for our character. Indeed our character is of infinitely greater importance in an eternal time scale (Mark 8:35).

So where do we go to seek right thinking and right motivation in all the complex web of social interactions that make up our lives? Jesus was asked precisely this question by the lawyer we read about in Mark 12:28 and Luke 10:25, and his amazingly brief reply could almost be regarded as a complete summing up of Exodus, Leviticus and Deuteronomy in the light of God's full revelation of himself in Christ. The greatest commandment, the lawyer was told, is full and total surrender to God. And when we accept this first commandment the second has an inevitability about it that is inescapable. If we make his purpose our will, his holiness the goal of our conscience, his truth the basis of our thinking and let his love motivate our response, then our love for other people will be a true reflection of God's love for them. But without that Godward orientation we cannot help but be egocentric. If the second commandment is separated from the first and used as the basis for community living, loving one's neighbours becomes an attempt to love someone only with all our own selfishness, inconsistencies and mixed motives. But if we first love the Lord God who has created us and our neighbour in his image, then however imperfectly we may reflect that image in practice, it sets the second commandment in an infinite perspective rather than just a limited human one.

Love for God is the prior and essential characteristic of the biblical covenant. Jesus did not come primarily as a social reformer or a healer, he came preaching repentance and the presence of the kingdom of God (Mark 1:14). When he met with the paralysed man he showed him clearly that it was more important that his sins were forgiven than that he should walk again (Mark 2:5). The prophets, while speaking out strongly against injustice and exploitation, clearly saw them primarily as offences against God and a breaking of covenant obligations (2 Samuel 12:1–12; 1 Kings 21). The uniqueness of the biblical covenant lies in this inter-relationship of the infinite and the finite, the eternal and temporal, the heavenly and the earthly.

It is still a fundamental principle for living as Christians in our technological world today.

8

Living as the people of God

We have been looking in considerable detail at the way our society is working, at some of the pressures for change and the stress that this causes. We have also attempted to look behind the familiar experiences to begin to understand the motivation, the system of belief, that is bringing this about. It has been suggested that a belief in the power of technology alone to bring us the good life, and the conviction that man is autonomous and at the controls of spaceship earth, is the base-line on which our society is built. This act of faith, this acceptance of a guiding philosophy has been called technicism. For the great majority of people it is not a conscious decision, they are being pushed along by the pressure of events. Nevertheless, it is important to try to understand why this is happening, because for so many people this technological world we have shaped is their total reality. They are living in a double-glazed society with man-made and man-limited horizons.

We have also looked at some biblical principles which run counter to this faith in technicism and at the record of God's dealings with his people, particularly in the idea of a covenant relationship between God and man. It is only too obvious that there is a great gulf between the aggressive, machine-minded and double-glazed society described in chapters 4, 5, 6 and a society being guided by covenant principles. The really fundamental difference is seen in the way truth is defined and in the authority that is accepted as final.

If we place man and his achievements at the centre of our world, then our values become selfish and relative and society becomes aggressive and unstable. If, on the other hand, we acknowledge that God is at the centre as an eternal reference point then our humanly defined priorities and the technological developments we are bringing about can always be referred back to him for assessment. This would not rule out adventure, change, and achievement but it would enable us to redirect our God-given motivation to subdue the earth and to enjoy it. If we held the truly biblical view of man as being made in the image of God and as steward of his creation then we would not continue to build our society on the assumption that man is just a machine and that the world just happens to be there to be exploited.

The challenge

Perhaps the greatest challenge for the church at the end of the twentieth century is to demonstrate its covenant faith to a society that does not understand the nature of its need. We have to learn how to live as the people of God in a high-tech world. The problem we face is not simply one of adapting to or resisting particular technological developments. Society is not being threatened by robots or computers. It is being isolated from God by an overwhelming faith in technicism. Just as the problem embraces the whole of life, so it can only be combatted with a faith which embraces the whole of life. The rest of this chapter looks at some of the reasons why we do not demonstrate this kind of faith very well and suggests some possible areas for local action.

There are no easy answers. We must humbly seek to understand God's purpose in putting us in today's technological world and be willing to stand under his authority as we seek guidance for action. I believe this will be done most effectively by small groups taking local action, using the roles and the gifts God has given. It is unlikely to be spectacular, it will not be highly organised or administratively tidy, but I would like to think that in hundreds of small local situations the value judgements of our society could be more effectively challenged by a Christian presence and a Christian voice.

Voting with our feet

When we start looking at how we should live, we immediately face the issue of 'separation versus involvement'. The question is sometimes raised in this form: if society has distanced itself from God so much that there is very little chance of a dialogue, if Christian concepts and language are completely foreign to the majority, if the accepted contemporary values are positively anti-Christian, then is it not time to come out and be separate? Surely we must avoid being contaminated by the evil influences prevalent in the world. Separation has been adopted by certain religious groups throughout history and has always been a minority practice of the Christian faith.

But there is another form of separation so widely practised today that it is accepted as normal. It is seldom a topic for discussion and even less frequently an area for action, so we do not even realise the extent to which it is stunting our faith and our witness to the world. This separation is an acceptance by Christians and by the rest of society of what has been called a sacred-secular divide. That is, we accept that religious ideas and questions are relevant in a few areas of life but that they have no part to play in most of our experiences.

Recent examples will make the existence of this dividing line obvious. On issues of life, death, marriage, abortion, euthanasia and divorce, church leaders and professionals in these areas have spoken out with a specifically Christian comment. Their views may not have carried much weight but were accepted as valid points of view. In the current national crises of unemployment, nuclear disarmament and AIDS there has also been Christian comment and this has almost always been followed by condemnation from politicians and media commentators because these subjects were not considered to come within the jurisdiction of a Christian critique.

The average Christian will not be speaking out on national issues in this way but the topics will inevitably come up in our homes and where we work. Our contribution to these debates, if made from the standpoint of Christian belief, will almost certainly be seen as invalid, because 'Christian belief' stands on the wrong side of the sacred-secular divide. In our technologically based society, separation has become the *de-facto* position for a large part of the church. There is a widespread feeling, for the most part unarticulated, that it could actually be spiritually risky to get too involved in some areas of life. Science, with its cool, analytical methods, seems to pose a destructive challenge to the Christian faith. Biblical accounts of creation, resurrection and God's control of the natural world are discounted. Theological compromise from some church leaders only serves to deepen the confusion. Many Christians are receiving the message that theology is in retreat, doctrines and beliefs held by the church for centuries are now being weakened, the secular side of the divide is growing larger, and the sacred side is getting smaller. Since scientific investigation and analysis respect no boundaries it seems generally safer to adopt a private and 'other-worldly' concept of the Christian faith rather than try to set it in the context of this present world.

Technology is the result of applying scientific methods to the problems of our lives. It comes with the authority of science, it is validated by its enormous success in increasing our standards of living and it is placed very definitely on the secular side of the divide. It does not pose such a direct challenge to our faith as do some scientific issues – the theory of evolution for example. But much more dangerously, technology is, with a few exceptions, assumed to be morally neutral and therefore to have no relevance for our Christian faith. There is almost no debate about the overwhelming technological base of our society and its influence on our thinking, our values and our relationships. We recognise the danger of materialism but not that of the ethics of technicism. So we have little to say on the secular side of the divide.

A demolition job

The idea of a division between the sacred and the secular is not a biblical one. Right through the Old Testament we see God concerned with every aspect of his people's lives. His covenant with Israel involved not only a call to worship but also a call to service: God's character was to be reflected in the way people lived their daily lives. When the prophets spoke out against injustice in the market place, abuse of political power and grossly unequal distribution of resources, they were expressing God's concern that his values should pervade all areas of life. But people still managed to split life into 'sacred' and 'secular' – bits they would let God have a say in, and bits where they would not. In Matthew 22:15–22 the Pharisees lined up on the 'sacred' side to challenge Jesus about paying taxes to Caesar. They had constructed for themselves a religious clique in which they tried to pretend that they could be uncontaminated by the world. In contrast, the Herodians were unashamedly collaborators with, and beneficiaries of, the Roman occupying power. These unlikely allies colluded in trying to make Jesus recognise a sacred-secular divide by coming down on one side or the other. Jesus' reply is the classic denial of the validity of any such concept. We have responsibilities, he says, both to God and to our fellow men; we live under the authority of God and under the authority of the local government. To opt out of either is a denial of our full duty to God.

Later on, before Pilate, Jesus again demolished this imaginary divide (John 19:11). He drew attention to the fact that Pilate was not autonomous in a 'secular' world. He was acting just as much under God's authority as were the Pharisees and Jesus himself.

The early church very soon erected its own version of this sacred-secular barrier and we find Paul writing to counter it. In Romans 12 he calls Christians to holiness – but in the context of using themselves and their gifts in God's service. They are not to conform to the pattern of this world but are not to opt out either. Rather they are to let their minds be *transformed* so that they live in the world with a different set of priorities. Certainly these priorities will involve service to our brothers and sisters in Christ but our Christian ministry is also extended to everyone with whom we are in contact (vs 17–21). This is to be the case both in our private and our public lives (13:1–7).

Paul's command is, 'Do not be overcome by evil; but overcome evil with good.' In Ephesians 6:10–18, Paul spells out that we are not to retreat from the world behind a defensive barrier. Rather, being 'clothed with Christ' we are to launch an offensive campaign against the devil's schemes (Romans 13:14).

New belt and braces

How can we begin to demolish this barrier in contemporary thinking? At the end of his confrontation with Ahab Elijah felt that he had failed; he was depressed and fearful (1 Kings 19:1–5). Despite the signs of God's power there had been no fundamental change in society. The Israelites had rejected God's covenant, broken down his altars and put his prophets to death. Elijah felt alone in a hostile world.

Most of us can appreciate his feelings as we go out to work in a society that knows nothing of God and ridicules those who believe in his active involvement in society. But we can also learn from Elijah's response in this situation. He went to Mount Horeb to stand in the presence of the Lord. We do need so very much to wait on the Lord so that he can renew our strength. We need to hear him encourage us in a gentle whisper, and teach us to choose our priorities correctly and courageously.

God sent Elijah back into Israel with the assurance that he was not alone, and with the practical instruction to seek support. Where today can we find the support which will help us to chip away at the dividing line in our society between sacred and secular?

First of all we must work for change within the church. It has, by and large, the wrong self-image, an unfortunate set of priorities, and organizational structures which reinforce the secular-sacred division. We will look at each of these in turn.

Wrong image

In Western Europe the church's relationship to the world is thought to be something like this:

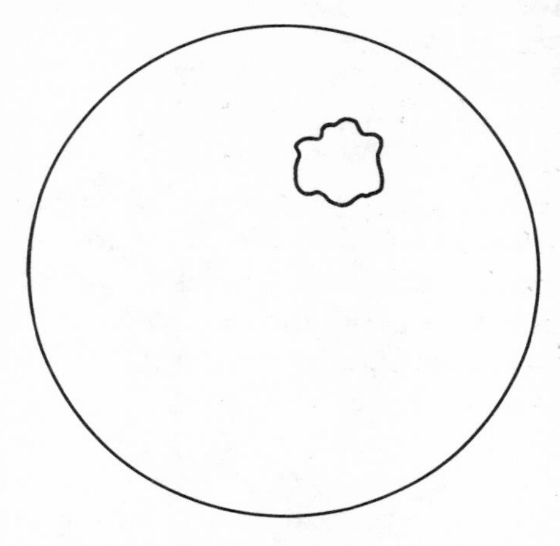

It is a tiny enclave, inhabited by a very small number of rather peculiar people. It used to cover a much bigger area but has been shrinking steadily since most of the reasons for its existence seem to have disappeared. There is of course no *physical* barrier around this enclave and those who consider themselves to belong inside in fact spend most of their lives outside. The great majority of people, who consider themselves to belong outside, are quite likely to pay occasional visits inside. However, when they do this they face problems as severe as a high physical wall – problems of language, different types of activities, a changed order of priorities.

Those who belong on the inside have a sense of mission, a desire to encourage other people to join them so that the enclave will expand. And they carry out this mission in one of two ways. One way is to beam propaganda across the enclave boundary, hoping that those outside will find it understandable and relevant. The other method is to organize sorties into the wider world in order to invite those belonging there to come and visit the enclave for a special reception party. Hopefully, when they meet these peculiar residents on home ground they will find they are really just the same as everybody else and will be attracted to join them.

Plainly this is a caricature, but I believe we do, too easily, see ourselves as a beleaguered minority struggling for survival, and we place far too much importance on the barricade we have erected around the enclave of the church. When Elijah had been up on the mountain he was soon sent down again by God to get involved in the unsavoury politics of Israel. We must begin to explore the idea that our mission may well be to live and work in the world. We would then think about the church in the world in terms more like the second diagram:

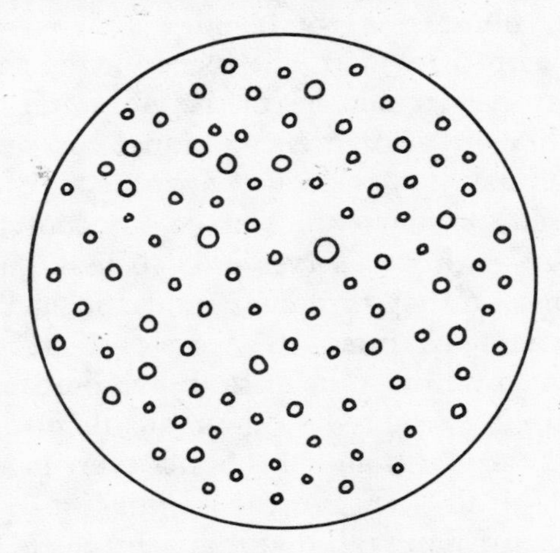

This may make you think of grains of salt shaken out over an omelette, or of tiny lights from scattered houses in a dark landscape, and there good precedents for such pictures.

Wrong priorities

In our more perceptive moments we in the church accuse ourselves of concentrating on maintenance rather than mission. Many of us know the frustration of realizing just how much time is taken up on buildings, finance and administrative planning and we wistfully speculate on what it would be like if we could travel light. But many local churches have inherited a heavy burden of these things for a wide variety of reasons. Some of them seem to be necessary but to monopolize an unreasonable share of our resources. Some seem indefensible but impossible to change.

In church life

The local situation is often reinforced by the top-heavy structure of the church at national level. I seriously question, for instance, the relevance of our cathedrals to the Church of England's mission to this country. They *can* be justified on a number of grounds: they are an irreplaceable heritage, they provide a unique focus for the church, and perhaps they even remind us of the glory and majesty of God. But they are also an encumbrance to the church in its mission in that they encourage a wrong set of priorities. The same can, of course, be true of any church building or symbol of faith if it serves only to make us inward-looking, concentrating on maintaining the enclave rather than encouraging us to face the needs of the technological world in which we live. The institutional bureaucracy and professional élite required to maintain them do little to help the average Christian in his or her everyday life. Most significantly of all, they present an image to the rest of society of a Christian faith that is anachronistic, ritualistic and irrelevant to daily life. They are the symbols *par excellence* of a church which shuts itself off from the pressures of a society pervaded by technicism.

In an emphasis on numbers

Yet in practice very few of us can ignore the pressures of our society. We naturally react against them by trying to feel more secure. One of the ways of doing this is to concentrate on numbers. This in itself is a way of reacting which reflects secular priorities. Many churches see as their main problem the falling numbers of those attending worship. Specialists in church growth would have us survey the parish or town, analyse the population groupings, plan a visiting campaign, organize follow-up and keep careful records. But Jesus said that the kingdom of God is like a seed growing to harvest. It is necessary to sow and to harvest but what happens in between is largely unknown to us and therefore out of our control. The kingdom of God is not going to be built by organizational planning. Perhaps we should learn a lesson from the large increase in the number of Christians in China during the period when the church as an institution was banned.

The wrong priority of numbers can even affect our prayer life. In Jesus' ministry prayer took place in small groups. Some prayer meetings today seem to be organized on the assumption that as many people as possible must be involved because the chances of success rise with the number of people praying. However, 'bigger is better' is not a biblical measure of success.

In Christian teaching

The theology we pursue and the Christian teaching we receive is often very selective and is not geared to helping us develop a full covenant faith for living as part of today's world. It often concentrates either on *personal* commitment and salvation, or on applying the gospel only in social terms: caring for the poor and needy. It is more demanding to apply biblical principles to our work and leisure, or to react with a positive Christian witness to some of the industrial and commercial pressures that influence our daily lives. We have a theology for living in the enclave but not for living out in the world.

Part of the reason for this is that those outside the church try to maintain the sacred-secular divide. For example, there was a hostile reaction from some politicians to the recent report, *Faith in the City*. The church, we were told, should concentrate on its own business of saving souls and not meddle in issues which are not its concern – such as bad housing and unemployment. There is, however, some hard thinking being done to work out biblical guidelines for practical action in today's world: the *Science, Religion and Technology Project* of the Church of Scotland is one example of this. But how often does this material filter down to local church level, stimulating discussion, provoking hard study and producing realistic, practical ways of application to our Christian witness?

Another reason for our lack of 'theology of the world' is that the theology we do have is too church-orientated and often exaggerates the importance of issues that are remote from most people's daily lives. To judge from the coverage in the press recently, the main topic of theological concern has been the question of whether or not to ordain women priests, while the moral issues raised by the arrival of AIDS seem to be ignored. For more years than most of us care to remember, high level discussions have been going on about church unity. But most of us, as Christians going about our everyday lives, are only too pleased to meet another Christian with similar attitudes and a similar faith! We have no difficulty in accepting a bond of unity that has already been forged by the Holy Spirit, and we are quite happy to worship with one another if the opportunity arises. It seems to be our church leaders, the theologians and spiritual professionals, who find formal church unity simultaneously so desirable to achieve and so difficult to bring about.

We do not need ecclesiastical hair-splitting theology; we do need a strengthened and expanded faith for everyday living. We need interpretations of biblical truth which will help us make decisions over practical issues. Such issues may arise, for example, out of society's changing social behaviour or the development of medical technology. We do not need detailed rules for living, nor does the Bible provide them. Rather it teaches us the meaning of life under a sovereign God and leaves us to make our own decisions in the light of that knowledge. The kingdom of God, says Paul, is not a matter of eating and drinking – of detailed, legalistic applications – but of righteousness, peace and joy in the Holy Spirit (Romans 14:17, 18).

We need, therefore, a theology for mission. We need to know what is implied by the fact that we are a chosen people, a royal priesthood, a holy nation, a people belonging to God. Peter expands this in 1 Peter 2–4. Making these chapters the basis of a six-month church education programme could be a revolutionary experience.

As we have already seen, attempts to demolish the sacred-secular divide often meet with harsh criticism and active resistance from both sides, so our mission to the society in which we live and work will often be frustrating. It will call for endurance, patience, as well as courage to be the uncomfortable presence which challenges worldly thinking. This is what our churches' priority should be; it is for this that our theology should equip us.

Wrong structures

In our thinking

We almost always see things as being 'spiritual' or 'non-spiritual'. Take, for example, an evening house group meeting. The leader has started off the discussion by putting a tin of baked beans on the table and asking what Christian associations it triggers in the minds of the group members. The replies will almost certainly be something like this:

- Harvest and God's promise.
- The work of farmers.
- The world of plenty and our use of it.
- Countries where there is starvation and our responsibility to them.

- The work of relief organizations.
- The ease and comfort of our lives, thanks to our industries.

It is much less likely that we would hear ideas such as:

- God's gifts in resources and skills in the mining and metal-processing industries.
- The work of engineers in inventing tractors.
- The benefits and dangers in our use of agricultural technology.
- The work of politicians in negotiating aid to under-privileged countries.
- The cheapness and variety of our food because of modern marketing and advertising methods.

In our view of ministry
The 'sacred-secular' divide also appears in the concept of 'full-time ministry' or 'full-time Christian service'. We seem to have a hierarchy of Christian work, a sort of spiritual pecking order which, in descending order of importance, would read something like this:

1. Full-time ordained ministry.
2. Other full-time ministry such as parish workers, evangelists, youth workers, overseas missionaries.
3. Part-time ministry such as lay assistants, music directors, administrators.
4. Work in para-church organizations such as youth movements, bookshops, missionary societies.
5. Work in secular jobs with some Christian associations, eg medicine, teaching, social work.
6. Spare time Christian work, such as Sunday school teaching, house group leadership, building maintenance, making tea, etc.

This statement is reinforced in practice by our prayer commitment. If you examine the prayer topics of your own church over a month or two, you will discover that the 'secular' activities on which ninety per cent of curch members spend ninety percent of their time just do not appear. Can it be that all this work does not need to be prayed for? There seems to be no concept that a Christian working in a bank, a shop, the local factory or the family home is engaged in full-time Christian service.

Is there a *non*-sacred ministry to which the majority of Christians are called? If not, then most of us would seem to be missing out on the greatest challenge we can ever face. If there is such a thing, we need to look into the biblical basis of these two aspects of ministry. Are they both ordained by God? If so, is the purpose directed towards different areas of service in the world? Are there really areas that can be labelled sacred and secular?

If our understanding is wrong, our witness in the world will be severely limited. If our view of the sacred ministry is one that sees it as the peak of Christian service then our brightest and best young Christians (provided they are male) will continue to be encouraged to separate themselves from the world to live and work within the church enclave. This may well enrich the life of the enclave but it also contributes to the spiritual deprivation in the worlds of industry, commerce, politics and education. Of course, Christians as a body do need people to lead, teach, exhort, visit, care, organize and administrate, and this takes time and needs special training, individual gifts and deep commitment. But if we delegate this work and the work of evangelising 'the world' to small groups of special people, the rest of us are abdicating our responsibilities. Our attitude is that of Moses when told by God to go to Pharaoh. 'Why me? What could I do? People wouldn't accept me. I haven't those sort of gifts, please send someone else.'

We are inextricably involved in this world. Its care is our covenant responsibility. There is no way in which we can opt for a self-sufficient, cosy church enclave. We cannot ignore the technological base of our culture by building ourselves an alternative environment which presents fewer challenges to our faith. On the contrary, it is time the church faced up to its wider responsibilities and made a positive attempt to speak with a prophetic voice in these areas of contemporary life.

9

Go into all the world

We have seen how our image of the church and the priorities which tend to result, reinforce a division between sacred and secular in our thinking. How can we correct this? The church's role is not an easy one. It was, after all, the first multinational conglomerate and suffers from many of the disadvantages of such very large organizations. Having said that, it is of course absolutely fundamental that the church's mission to the world should follow the pattern set by its Lord. The emphasis must be on individual faith and commitment, personal evangelism and witness and the healing ministry to those in need. It must also have a concern for justice in all situations of oppression and be prepared to speak out against any grossly unequal sharing of resources. The evidence that the Messiah has come is still that the blind receive sight, the lame walk, those who have leprosy are cured, the deaf hear, the dead are raised, and the good news is preached to the poor (Matthew 11:5).

To do this more effectively today we will have to widen our view of mission. *Every* member of the church should be enrolled into 'full-time ministry', making the best use of their talents and interests in their place of work, in their leisure activities, in their homes and with their local community. We have to make a serious attempt to challenge the value systems derived from our technological thinking. We should be engaged in a preventative ministry as well as a healing one.

With very few exceptions this seems to be unexplored territory. We will need to take a new look at the resources of the local church: the experience and knowledge of all those people who spend most of their time producing the goods and services we need. They are grappling at first hand with the excitement and the stress of technological change. How does this challenge their faith? What compromises are they making? What support do they need? Can they exert any degree of Christian influence? We do not know because we have not asked.

Living dangerously

Moving out in this way will mean living more dangerously. A Christian voice is not welcome on the secular side of the divide. But if we believe that the world is still in a covenant relationship with God then, even if the idea is rejected by the great majority, it is vital that they are not allowed to ignore the fact. As disciples of Christ we are commanded to go into the world to reflect a little of God's glory.

It is a world which groans under the weight of its own pain. Attempting to influence the value systems of individuals or society is much harder than picking up the broken pieces; but unless we do exert this influence the broken pieces will increase and overwhelm us.

Working with other Christians will involve a clash of theological backgrounds and differing interpretations of biblical truth – a much more difficult situation than working only in our own, highly selective, church fellowship. Working with non-Christians will lead us into compromising situations. We will have to make decisions in areas where there are no clear-cut answers, only choices between the lesser of evils. We need help to know where to draw a line and where to stick on a principle. The decisions we will take or agree to will perhaps be condemned from the study desk and also, quite possibly, by God. Dietrich Bonhoeffer faced an appalling decision because of his involvement in the plot to assassinate Hitler. He is quoted as saying:

> 'The free responsibility of free men depends on a God who demands bold action as the free response of faith and who promises forgiveness and consolation to the man who becomes a sinner in the process.'

Taking action

Inevitably, this book's concluding call to action will be a very open-ended one. There is no blueprint for moving out into the world; there are no models for this mission. Every local situation is different so we cannot expect to copy the experience of others, but we can learn from them and be encouraged by what they are trying to do. At the end of the book is a short list of source material which can be used to follow up some of the ideas I have been discussing. There are addresses of organizations which are attempting to stimulate and support local initiatives. The list is by no means comprehensive. Regard it as a starter pack to be added to as you go along. The real work must always be done at local level, by small groups of people with a common interest and commitment. They are the only people who are aware of the local needs and who can act directly and relevantly in a local situation. They will be personally involved in working out the consequences of any decisions; this ensures some serious thinking and assessment of the results.

We are called as Christians to live transformed lives in this world. We should campaign with renewed minds as well as with our hearts. This is much more demanding than simply putting our name to a petition or joining a mass movement. We must decide, in our small local groups, what are the real issues of practical and spiritual importance in our community and seek God's guidance about the way we should try to influence them.

Without suggesting an order of priority, I would like to illustrate some of the possible directions such projects might take.

Education: battleground for the next generation

In our schools today there is an increasing difference between secular and Christian teaching. Curriculum developments discriminate in favour of the former and against the latter. I am not referring here to specifically Christian instruction. There is a very good case to be made that this should take place in the Christian family. Rather, I am talking about the philosophy which motivates those who are in responsible positions in our education system. The curriculum, which is increasingly being specified by central authority, is based on reductionist thinking and assumes that a scientific analysis of the facts will lead to the total truth. The majority of those who teach acquiesce in this philosophy, even if they do not fully realise it, because it is a fundamental part of the culture of our age and society. In contrast, our teaching about anything can only be true to reality when it is based on a respect for whole truth, and shows a real humility before the facts in whatever form they are received. Thus, teaching mathematics, music, science or literature should be a Christian vocation and the way we teach should reveal our philosophy.

How well does your church support the Christian teachers in its local schools? Our schools are the battle-ground for the next generation. We should therefore expand our concept of mission in our local area by deliberately trying to concentrate a Christian influence in them. This is one way in which we might effectively challenge the predominant thinking and assumptions of a society brought up on technicism. Has any small group of churches made a long-term commitment to work and pray for the Christian members of staff of a local school – or for more Christian teachers to move into the school? Have we considered what a revolutionary effect this could have on the quality of education for those children? Do we even believe it is possible? Militant political groups have shown how easy it can be to gain a position of influence in sensitive areas of public life. It is also part of the church's missionary calling.

Parents as well as teachers are closely involved in education policy. The 1986 Education Act gives significant new powers to school governors. As Christian parents we need to organize ourselves to ensure that our voice is heard in influencing school policy. Other groups are already attempting to do this and we may well discover that they are advocating policies that are contrary to God's word, especially in the fields of sex education and family life. Where does this issue come on a Christian parent's priority list compared with membership of the PCC or teaching in Sunday school? For some of us, perhaps it should be our main area of work for Christ.

Work: covenantal stewardship

We have seen that most of us live divided lives, splitting our time and energies between two cultures. We tend to accept a different value system, have different aims, and even speak a different language on the two sides of the sacred-secular divide. Many Christians do not seriously consider their paid employment, or that which occupies a major slice of their lives, in spiritual terms. Peter Challen, of the South London Industrial Mission, has introduced the concept of a 'theological audit' to try to break through this barrier.

Such an audit is an attempt to account for our stewardship of the talents and resources given us by God. We can start by asking ourselves how our faith affects our witness for Christ in our personal or private life, in our public or working life, and in our life as a citizen of the country and of the world. We will almost certainly find it difficult to reconcile our Christian witness in all three areas. The second area is usually the one in which we find most problems. This audit will immediately raise two questions about our working lives. Firstly, what decisions and problems do we face? Secondly, how do we see our faith relating to these problems and decisions?

The biblical ideal of work is something which is good, a reflection of the character of God the creator. Very dimly, most people will experience this in their hobbies and DIY activities. But it is much more rarely to be found in their paid employment. There it is only too obvious that we live in a fallen world. Where the unifying leadership of Christ is rejected, the various aspects of a person's life will gradually work themselves out of step with each other, resulting in the frustrations and tensions with which we are familiar. For many people, work either becomes status-seeking and career oriented, or is meaningless, insulting, impersonal and mechanistic.

We have a duty to explore these issues together, supporting each other as we question and, if need be, try to change products and working methods. The world of work desperately needs Christians with technical and managerial experience who can think and speak with the right blend of professional authority, and submission to the guidance of the Holy Spirit. It needs to be done in works meetings and trades union committees, on boards of management and in technical development discussions.

It might seem idealistic to attempt to challenge the assumptions behind an industrial or commercial organization, but it has been done successfully. George McRobie, in his book *Small is Possible*, gives a directory of industries where this challenge has been made. It ranges from the work of the Combined Shop Stewards' Committee of Lucas Aerospace to some local village community initiatives. Work conducted as if people matter can be shown to be a practical proposition as well as being closer to God's purpose for us as stewards of his world.

Government: making real God's promises

Submission to authority for the Lord's sake is commanded in the New Testament. (See, for example, 1 Peter 2:13.) In a democracy, however imperfect, this should take the form of an active co-operation in the processes of government. If we are stewards by God's command then his provident care is, in part, vested in us. We have a duty to participate at the foundation level of democracy, which is in the relationship between constituencies and their elected representatives in local or national government. How can we do this in a more positive way than just visiting the polling station? Most obviously, channels of communication must be opened up between the local Christian community and their councillors and member of Parliament. There is a need for a Christian point of view to be put and defended by reasoned argument. There is an equal need for Christians to understand the compromises that are inevitable in any political decision, and for a God-given wisdom to know when to stand fast on basic biblical principles. Not every Christian should get involved in party politics, but we must make a serious effort to raise a Christian voice and to put forward biblical values in the early stages of political decision making.

One way of doing this is to form a local pressure group which could interview its political leaders on specific current issues, write to the local press, circulate the neighbourhood with relevant information, and conduct local polls. In this way we can generate an awareness that behind political decisions there are assumptions about the nature and needs of man, as well as moral questions which need to be answered. When such a group reports back to local churches with their findings, those churches would become more aware of the importance and complexity of the issues. This would make some of our prayers more faithful and better informed, and begin to make a small breach in the church's side of the sacred-secular dividing wall.

These illustrations of ways in which we can move out into the world are primarily intended to stimulate thinking rather than be guidelines for action. But I think there are at least two general principles that should guide all our Christian work of this kind.

The first is that we are not called to take on half a dozen extra activities. Christ did not come that we might have meetings and have them more abundantly. He calls us to engage in *mission* more *relevantly*. So we must be prepared for a drastic re-assessment of what is, for many of us, a traditional Christian programme. The agenda for mission to a technological society might turn out to be quite different from the mission agendas to which we are accustomed.

Secondly, our choice of a specific mission field will depend on the people who are going to be involved, their knowledge and experience and the particular situations in which they live. Where we are is where we must engage. Whatever we choose to do we must strive for excellence, be better informed, have more relevant experience, express a wider concern and bring more compassion than those with whom we contend. In those ways we can raise a

Christian voice in a technological world, in the name of Christ.

Works cited

Albury and Schwartz, *Partial Progress*, London, The Pluto Press, 1982.
Michael Allaby, *Inventing Tomorrow*. London, Hodder and Stoughton, 1976.
Stuart Blanch, *The Sound of the Trumpet in the Morning*. London, Hodder and Stoughton, 1979.
Campbell Campbell-Jack, *A Nuclear Babel? Third Way Magazine*, April 1986.
Faith in the City; A Call for Action by Church and Nation: Report of the Archbishop of Canterbury's Commission on Urban Priority Areas. London, Church House Publishing, 1985.
Frederick Forsyth, *The Devil's Alternative*, London, Corgi, 1979.
John Gribben, *In Search of the Big Bang: Quantum Physics and Cosmology*. London, Heinemann, 1986.
James Houston, *I Believe in the Creator*. Grand Rapids, Eerdmans, 1987.
Ivan Illich, *Tools for Conviviality*. London, Calder and Bayers, 1973.
Paul Johnson, *Enemies of Society*. London, Weidenfeld and Nicolson, 1977.
Hans Kung, *On Being a Christian*. London, Collins, 1977.
David Lyon, *Mules, Mills and Micros. Third Way Magazine*. January 1984.
Donald Mackay, *The Clockwork Image*, Leicester, IVP, 1974.
George McRobie, *Small is Possible*. London, Jonathan Cape, 1981.
Vance Packard, *The People Shapers*. London, MacDonald and James, 1978.
Martin Pawley, *The Private Future*. London, Thames and Hudson, 1973.
E F Schumacher, *Good Work*. London, Jonathan Cape, 1979.
B F Skinner, *Beyond Freedom and Dignity*. London, Bantam Press, 1972.
Alvin Toffler, *The Third Wave*. London, Jonathan Cape, 1979.
Paul Tournier, *The Gift of Feeling*. London SCM, 1981.
Peter Ueberroth, *Made in America*. New York, William Morrow, 1985.
H G Wells, *Penguin Book of English Short Stories*, Harmondsworth, Penguin, 1958.

Further reading

John Atkinson, *The Media – A Christian View*. London, Epworth Press, 1979.
Fred Catherwood, *The Christian In Industrial Society*. Leicester, IVP, 1980.
David Field and Elspeth Stephenson, *Just The Job*. Leicester, IVP, 1978.
John Gladwin, *God's People In God's World*. Leicester, IVP, 1979.

Charles Martin, *You've Got To Start Somewhere: The Christian in Education*. Leicester, IVP, 1979.
Stephen Monsma (ed), *Responsible Technology*. Grand Rapids, Eerdmans, 1986.
Malcolm Muggeridge, *Christ And The Media*. London, Hodder and Stoughton, 1977.
Francis Schaeffer, *The Church At The End Of The Twentieth Century*. London, Hodder and Stoughton, 1970.
Alan Storkey, *A Christian Social Perspective*. Leicester, IVP, 1979.
A N Triton, *Whose World?* Leicester, IVP, 1978.
Mary Whitehouse, *Mightier than the Sword*. Eastbourne, Kingsway, 1985.

Resource material for local groups

Resource materials can be obtained from the following organizations.

CARE Campaigns, 21a Down Street, London, W1Y 7DN.
Information and advice on local action, particularly in political and educational areas.

The Evangelical Alliance, 186 Kennington Park Road, London SE11 4BT.
Together with the Bible Society the Evangelical Alliance publishes the *UK Christian Handbook*, ed. Peter Brierly. This is a well-indexed reference book giving details of hundreds of organizations who are supporting Christian mission in the widest sense. The Evangelical Alliance will also be able to give you information about its *Evangelical Enterprise* project. This scheme has been set up to fund, on a fifty-fifty basis with the government, development work in inner city areas.

Grove Booklets, Bramcote, Nottingham, NG9 3DS.
Catalogue available covering a wide range of ethical studies on current issues.

Shaftesbury Project, 8 Oxford Street, Nottingham, NG1 5BH.
Information packs and group discussion material on various areas of social concern.